The Two-Minute Drill to Manhood

A Proven Game Plan For Raising Sons

By John Croyle

ADVANCED READER'S COPY

TEXT AND INTERIOR DESIGN NOT FINAL

978-1-4336-8071-7

Published by B&H Publishing Group
Nashville, Tennessee

Dewey Decimal Classification: TO COME
Subject Heading: TO COME

Unless otherwise noted, Scripture quotations are taking from the New American Standard Bible (NASB), © the Lockman Foundation, 1960, 1962, 1963, 1968, 1971, 1972, 1973, 1975, 1977; used by permission.

I've made a lot of mistakes as a man, husband, and father; perhaps you have, too. There came a time in my life when I decided to draw a line in the sand and grow up. Thankfully, it's never too late for any of us to change.

Dedication

This book is dedicated to the next generation—Cade, Will, Sawyer, and Gibbs—who are now learning to be good men from our son and son-in-law.

Acknowledgments

To ALL of the children who have called Big Oak Ranch their home since 1974 who have taught all of us much more than we ever taught them.

This book is the culmination of countless hours our front-line warriors, the houseparents at Big Oak Ranch, and our support staff have put into our children to mold them into the quality young adults that God intended them to be.

Thank you to Susan Doyle for helping put all of these years of experience of raising children into an understandable, usable, transferrable format.

Contents

Preface

Instruct them to do what is good, to be rich in good works,
to be generous, willing to share, storing up for themselves
a good reserve[a] for the age to come, so that they may take
hold of life that is real. (1 Timothy 6:18–19)

If you are the parent of a teenager, whether you realize it or not, you are coming down to what I call the two-minute drill. The two-minute drill is best known as those last two minutes of a football game—and they are crucial. Those two minutes don't diminish the rest of the game. In fact, the rest of the game builds to these few moments, and they so often determine the final outcome of the game.

The first quarter begins with the opening kickoff. Your adrenalin is pumping. Your stomach is full of butterflies. It's the beginning of the game. You're facing new competition and challenges. You've watched hours of film, and you're finally face-to-face with the guy lined up across from you. He may be bigger or stronger than you, but your job is to figure out how to beat him. The first time you hit him, you might think, *Whoa! He is a lot stronger than I thought.* So, you have an opportunity to adjust right there, on the fly, to begin with, knowing you can't fight with him during the entire game. You know that you've got to out-quick him, out-smart him, out-last, out-whatever to win.

The second quarter comes. You're moving toward those five minutes just before the end of the second quarter. The score at the end of the second quarter doesn't determine who wins or loses—only the end of the second half does that. But the last five minutes of the second quarter are key because that's when your first half momentum finishes up and leads into halftime, when you make necessary adjustments.

Then comes the third quarter. In the first five minutes, that guy in front of you knows, *Hey! He adjusted. He's playing differently. He's approaching or angling for me differently from the way he did in the first half.* Or, *He's running this route this way when before it was another way.* Or, *the quarterback changed tactics because he read the linebacker and knows that his opponent is a step slower than he was at the first of the game.*

The fourth quarter rolls around, specifically the last two minutes of the fourth quarter. Every successful high school, college, and NFL team in America sets aside time in every week's preparation and practice for the two-minute drill in readiness for the weekend's game. Unless the game ends up in a lopsided score, this is a very critical part of the game that will determine whether the team wins or loses. These last two minutes in the football game are when everything you have worked for—pre-season, August two-a-day practices, the game itself—boils down to your execution in those last two minutes. Imagine you've got to drive 80 yards in two minutes. Everybody's got to be on the same page, doing the same thing, applying everything they've learned.

The two-minute drill is played differently from the rest of

the ballgame. You might miss your block in the second quarter, third series, and second down play. That's okay. You might even have another chance to make up for that mistake. But, imagine that you miss a block in the two-minute drill, and the guy you were supposed to block sacks your quarterback. Your mistake means lost time and opportunity. You're losing valuable seconds of those last two minutes. It is so sad and so frustrating to watch the clock tick down as the quarterback is trying to get everybody up on the line of scrimmage for one last chance to score but time runs out. You lose, and, more importantly, the team loses. And you were so close to winning. Unfortunately, our country is now settling for just being that close to winning when it comes to producing a real man. You and I don't have to settle for nearly winning.

Winning a ballgame takes preparation, not just athletic ability. All the practice you have had prepares you to execute the play that you know will get the ball over the goal line to score. There is no second chance to get it right. You have one shot at it, and you must make it your best if you expect to win.

When our son, Brodie, who spent five years in the NFL, was in the ninth grade he was playing quarterback on the Westbrook Christian High School football team. It was the final drive of the semi-final game to determine if our team would go to Legion Field in Birmingham to play in the Super Six State High School Championship game. The head coach looked at this fourteen-year-old boy who was playing with 18-year-old young men and said, "They know you're a good quarterback. Let's show them you're a great one. Are you ready? Let's go."

Because they had practiced countless hours for this opportunity in the game, they drove the length of the field and scored as the final buzzer went off. Westbrook won the game and got to play for the state championship.

If you are the parent of a sixtten-year-old, the final seconds of the two-minute drill is where you are, right now. Time is running out and you are terrified your son or daughter isn't ready. The day God gives us that blessing called a child, click, the clock starts counting down, and the urgency of building and preparing for the two-minute drill in a football game is just like building and preparing for the urgency you face when that baby turns 16. Have you taught your son what it means to be a man? Have you taught your daughter what to look for in her future husband?

I encourage you to circle your child's high school graduation date on your calendar and then count back to today's date and mark it. That's how many days you have to prepare them for life. Is your game plan ready? If not, it's late, yes, but it's not too late.

This book, based on the practical experience I've had with my own son and daughter and with the 1,800-plus children who have been raised at Big Oak Boy's and Girl's Ranch, is actually a game plan for getting your child ready for the two-minute drill of life. It's important to have a good game plan. You must execute it as perfectly as possible, checking with God daily. You must be diligent in planning, preparation and practice. You must stay focused and never let your "team" doubt that you know exactly where you're going. When you finish the game and your children leave you to go out on their own, you will be able to rest assured you have done your best, your children will respect you, and you will know that you prepared them for the game of life because you prepared them for that two-minute drill.

The clock is ticking.

Chapter 1

The Game Plan

When our now-grown son, Brodie, was about thirteen years old, I called him at home one day and told him that when I got home that night we were going to talk about the two of us going on a "transition" trip.

"I'm going to take you somewhere, and we're going to talk about what it means to be a man," I told him. I was thinking some place local. That night when we talked, I learned Brodie was thinking Alaska. Obviously my budget to go somewhere local was not going to cover a trip to Alaska. It was a big dream, and I was willing and trusting to see how God might work it out.

Afterward, I was flying back through Dallas/Ft. Worth airport from a speaking engagement in California, waiting for my flight to Birmingham. As I walked up to the gate, the agent behind the desk announced, "If you'll give up your seat on this airplane, we'll give you a ticket to any place our airline flies within the United States." To sweeten the deal she also said, "If you will give us your ticket on this flight, we'll

get you back home fifteen minutes earlier on another flight."
I nearly broke that woman's arm trading with her right there.
It was a quick deal because I didn't want her to change her
mind! There was a very nice older woman behind me in the
line who also took the offer. Because we were transferred to
the same flight, we left the area and went to wait in a nearby
restaurant for our new flight.

We began talking about our good fortune. She asked,
"What are you going to do with your ticket?"

"My son and I are going to go on a trip to Alaska," I told
her.

She said, "Oh!" That was all the ticket talk we had at the
time.

When we finally got on our flight, we discovered that we
had adjoining seats, and immediately returned to our conversation. She asked, "Didn't I see you on a TV show recently?"

"Yes, ma'am, you did," I responded.

She then said, "I know about you! You used to play football for Coach Bryant."

"Yes, ma'am, I did in the early 70s. He was a great man
and coach. It was a joy to play for him. "

"I'm from Jasper, and my husband is the postmaster
there," she said, sharing more about herself. "Guess who my
best friend is?"

"I don't know," I responded.

"Mary Harmon." Her best friend was Mary Harmon
Bryant, Coach Paul "Bear" Bryant's wife. She continued, "She
has told me about you and what you do for the children at
the ranch."

Mrs. Bryant knew all about the plans I had for a children's ranch because while I was in college, she and I had had
a "date" every Friday of the football season at 3 o'clock in

the afternoon. Because Coach Bryant was such a far-ranging thinker, he always insisted that when the football team traveled to games, if he traveled on an airplane or bus, she traveled on a different airplane or bus. He felt that if the plane was to crash or the bus to wreck, their children would at least have one of their parents survive. So, I always traveled on whichever plane or bus Mrs. Bryant was on and sat in the seat next to her. The way I figured it, if God was going to take one of them, it wasn't going to be her! We visited for 36 Friday afternoons on the bus or the plane. Truly, she was an extraordinary woman and a really good friend to me.

During one of those early road trips, she asked me what I was going to do after college and football. I told her about the dream God had given me to start a home for children needing a chance. Children that are orphaned, abused, abandoned, neglected, or homeless. She was a great encourager during those days when most everyone else thought I had lost my mind. She believed in me and believed in my dream, and I will always be grateful for the support she gave to me.

So, here I was years later on a plane sharing this new "dream" of traveling to Alaska with Mrs. Bryant's friend.

I had decided to try to make Brodie's dream trip to Alaska happen, but I still wasn't sure how we would afford the trip. About three or four weeks before we were supposed to leave, I still had only the one ticket. I decided to call my new friend in Jasper and ask her if she would be willing to sell me her ticket.

She remembered our conversation about the trip I planned to take with Brodie. Before I could ask her about her ticket, she asked me, "Do you have your other ticket yet?"

"No, not yet," I told her.

For a greatly reduced price, she sold me her ticket. So, Brodie and I got to go to Alaska and back on essentially two free tickets. It worked out really, really well and the money we paid for her ticket was well worth it. The transportation was covered. Boy was I excited.

About a week or two before we were supposed to go, I still didn't know exactly what Brodie and I were going to talk about other than I knew we were going to talk about manhood and what it is. I didn't have a clue how the Lord wanted me to cover the topic.

The first thought that came to mind was, *I'm going to charge my son with being a man. C.H.A.R.G.E.* Six letters using acronyms like *C*hristlikeness, *H*eart for God, *A*ttitude, etc. It was easy to think up all of the cute little things that would fit, but that was just me trying to work out something instead of trusting God to show me His vision. Through the years, I have stubbornly learned that God really likes it when we ask Him to show us the way to follow His path. He wasn't going to do it for me, but He was waiting for me to ask Him to lead me as opposed to me stepping out on my own.

Another week passed and I was still wrestling with exactly what I was going to talk about with Brodie. On a Saturday morning at 4:55 just a few days before our planned departure, a voice spoke in my heart and said, *"Get up!"* I know what you're thinking; *He hears voices and thinks God is speaking to him!* If I were you, that's what I would be thinking!

At the time, we lived on the boys' ranch and my office was there, too. I got up and walked to my office. In my heart I kept repeating the question, *what do you want to teach your son about manhood?*

Again, I answered, "I want to charge him to be a man." *C.H.A.R.G.E.*

The voice came back and said again, *what do you want to teach your son about manhood?*

It hit me. *M.A.N.H.O.O.D.* Seven letters. That was it!

What I want to share in this book is what God gave me in about 30 seconds on that morning. It was one of those times when there wasn't a doubt in my mind what God was telling me to do. I couldn't have thought this entire thing up on my own. Everything I will share is what I used with my own son and daughter and with more than 1,800 boys and girls we've raised on the Big Oak Ranch.

It's easy to see how this book applies to boys, but everything here is applicable to both boys and girls. We all want to lead our sons to be men, but we also want to lead our daughters to know what to look for as they choose their spouse. Think about the fact that the young man your daughter chooses to marry will take care of your "princess" for the rest of her life. He'll be the father of your grandchildren. Like it or not, he'll show up at every family holiday and special occasion. We all want to know that we have taught our daughters to choose wisely. We cannot sit back and hope any of our children will find the way by trial and error. It's up to us to teach what it is to be a godly man or to choose one as a husband.

They say that experience is the best teacher. I've had the opportunity to experience coaching the two-minute drill with hundreds of boys and girls. I write this book so that other parents can benefit from those experiences in preparing for their own children's two-minute drill.

Start with Yourself

As parents, we must know who we are, what we are, and why we're here. Those are three bedrocks of parenting. They are just like the three sides of a pyramid or three legs of a stool.

If two sides are the same length and the third is different, we will always be out of balance.

Who Are You?

The movie *Secretariat* told the story of a horse that had all kinds of potential. One of the best lines in the movie was when the horse was born and stood almost immediately. The trainer looked over at the handler and asked him if he had ever seen anything like it. The handler said he'd never seen a colt stand that quickly. They knew right then that they had something special. Our sons are special, just like that horse. Our task as parents is to find, recognize, train, and develop that specialness.

As a parent, some of us are members of a two-parent team. We are co-coach to this child as we are raising them with our spouse. Some parents are single and face this task alone. However, we can choose others to help us—a baseball coach, a Sunday school teacher, a pastor, an uncle, an aunt, a wise grandfather, or a grandmother who is the picture of love. Whether as a married couple or as a single parent, we all should be our child's trainer and encourager.

As parents we must realize that each child is special in his or her own way and that each child has his or her own potential. Not everyone is going to be Secretariat. Some might just be an old Clydesdale pulling the wagon. But you know what? A parent can train a Clydesdale to be the best dog-gone, wagon-pulling Clydesdale that has ever been.

I would have loved to be a Secretariat, but I wasn't and I'm not. I'm just an old Clydesdale. I know who I am, my strengths and my weaknesses. The Bible says that young men stumble badly. I've been there, done it, and seen it. Even to this day, I will stupidly stumble or repeat something simply because I didn't learn the lesson. Our Heavenly Father is still teaching us the things that we need to do better, even when stubbornness still rules.

Who we are also depends on the imprinting we received from our parents and other mentors. There is not one of us who, while growing up, didn't make the statement, "I'll never do that to my kids when I grow up," or, "I'll never say that to my kids." We all have those pre-parenting absolutes that we embraced. But, then that horrible day has come for all of us when we heard the tone, the words, identified the attitude, and even used the same inflection we heard while growing up but swore to never do. There is a built-in, innate imprinting we each get from our parents.

Sometimes we repeat the negatives as well as the positives. The great parents I know weed out the negatives and focus on the positives. From the day I was born, my dad was always telling me one-liner nuggets of wisdom. He would say things like, "If you're going to do something, do it right." His exact words were sometimes a little more colorful, but they got the point across. Unfortunately, some parents are full of and focus only on negative one-liners such as "Can't you ever do anything right?" "Are you always going to be a loser?"

Mental, emotional, and physical orphans will repeat what they have experienced. If a person has been told all of his or her life, "Why can't you be more like (fill in the blank)," that person is forever imprinted with doubt and negativity. According to a quote from Edmund Burke, the foolish parent repeats history. Albert Einstein also said, "Insanity is doing the same thing over and over again and expecting different results." If it did not work with us, why would we want to repeat it with our own children?

A wise parent will realize how he or she differs from

the child and who God made that child to be. A wise parent will also ask for the wisdom that comes only from God and will apply the positive imprinting received from parents and mentors while filtering out the negative.

What Are You?

We've talked about who a parent is. Let's talk about who a parent is not. A parent is not the child's best friend, not their buddy, not their servant, not their enabler, not their defender at all costs, and not a liar or excuser on their behalf. A parent is not a protector against the other parent. Parents have to be on the same page. However, if, as a parent, you are protecting your child from the destructive abuse of a mate, you have a serious issue that should be addressed immediately. There are exceptions to this protector thing. If you are married to an alcoholic man and every time he walks in he slaps your son, you must protect your child. If your wife is verbally abusive to your daughter, you've got to be your daughter's protector. Any form of physical or emotional abuse will negatively imprint your child, eventually killing the child's spirit. None of us desire this for our children. At Big Oak Ranch, we have seen repeatedly the result of this type of abuse. The results are never good. We've also dealt with physical abuse, but the cycle can be broken.

I asked one little boy who came to live at the ranch why his dad had beaten him. The boy said, "I stood in front of my mom and told my daddy that he wasn't going to hit her anymore. So, then he started beating me."

"What your dad did was wrong," I told the boy. "What you did was right. You did what real men do; defend your mom at all cost."

Unfortunately, we've heard this story more times than we

care to count. But the good news is the boys can recover and become good men because they learn to focus on what they did right and not on what someone else did wrong.

As parents, we are not in the cloning business, reproducing ourselves. It's great to try to build into our children the positive qualities and strengths we have, but we're not trying to make them fit into a mold that looks like us. We should not force our children into molds to be something they are not. They need separate, unique molds. The best way I know to describe it is to look at the different forms of concrete. Wet concrete is poured into a form. That form can be built to be any shape, but once the concrete is poured and hardens with each passing minute it's pretty much set. After 18 years, a child is set, too. The only way to change them is to break them, and no one wants to do that. Our goal is to design the best possible form in which to mold them. So, parents are, in reality, form builders.

We are also decision makers. In the beginning of a child's life, the parent is 100 percent the decision maker—deciding what will be eaten, what will be worn, and what activities will be pursued. As the child gets older, they make more and more choices. The parent's role becomes more of a trainer. With each passing day, our influence on their decisions diminishes.

Recently, four boys from the ranch joined me on a duck hunt in Mississippi with Brodie. We were at Brodie's home and he and the boys were talking. My wife chimed in and said something to the effect of, "Yeah, you've always been stubborn and set in your ways." Brodie, as he was walking away, looked back over his shoulder and respectfully said, "No, Ma'am, y'all trained me to be my own man." It was priceless as far as I was concerned because that is what we trained him to be.

Both of our children left home at the age of seventeen. They were young, but it was time for them to start making their own decisions. Thankfully, they did well. So many kids' crash and burn that first year away from home because they don't know how to make wise decisions. By being an example in front of them, we as parents can teach them how to make wise decisions once they are on their own. Off-the-cuff, flippant decisions don't normally work so well, which leads me to the next aspect of being a parent. We should be thinkers and planners, not reactionaries nor blind leaders.

Short-term effects are usually easy to see. The long-term effects of decisions have to be based on wisdom and what I call the "eternal factor." As parents we train ourselves to think in terms of how will this decision affect my family long-term and more importantly, eternally. It doesn't come naturally, and it takes practice.

We are also adjustors, never compromising on the absolutes, but adjusting when we see areas where our children will benefit from a change. Proverbs 22:6 says, "Train up a child in the way he should go, even when he is old he will not depart from it." I know the Bible says we are not to add to any verse, but I think in today's parenting we could say, "Train up a child in the way he should go and when he is old *he might stray, but* he won't depart."

Our children *will* sometimes make bad choices, but we can make sure the foundation is there for them to come back to. Think back to the Prodigal Son. He went to the bottom but knew he could go back home. If there had not been a foundation built within him, it wouldn't have turned out the way it did. Yes, he messed up, but he came back to his senses because of the foundation.

A lot of good principles can be found in the management

of horses. There have been thoroughbred horses whose hearts have exploded because they were trying so hard to win. We have to be careful that we don't push our children so hard that their hearts "explode," but remember that training is hard and it works. It's not a one-moment instant thing. It's a continuous manual we write with our child. We just have to make sure, as the parent, we are the author, not them.

Why Are We Here?

The day your first child is born, your stomach is full of butterflies as you realize this child is relying totally on you. The opportunities are endless. That child cannot do anything alone and is 100 percent dependent on you. By the time your child is six or seven, your job is down to about 80 percent because now they are able to be somewhat independent from you in some areas of life. By the time they are 16, your job is 85 to 90 percent finished. The moment they get a driver's license, everything changes. Your role shifts to fine-tuning. They are both able and anxious to make choices on their own. Don't let it take you by surprise or let this time in your child's life and yours sneak up on you! Don't be the parent who sits at high school graduation crying because you are scared spitless that your child isn't ready. You can make sure they are.

When the score in a football game is close, you know that during those last two minutes, you've got to get down the length of the field. Every play, every movement, and every assignment is magnified. During the two-minute drill, you can't give up the ball. You've got to do everything you can to keep the ball in order to score. Every down is like a crucial fourth and goal play. You use every play to get a first down so that you maintain possession of the ball. Our relationship with our children is the same. Many times we say, oh, it's just one down, or missed opportunity, but let me elaborate.

Charles Francis Adams Jr., was a member of the prominent Adams family that produced two American presidents. As a little boy he wrote in his journal on a particular date that his dad took him fishing and referred to it as a wonderful day, certainly one not wasted. His father, on that same date, entered that he went fishing with his son and referred to it as a wasted day. Parenting is a matter of perspective. We get to choose our perspective for the game and especially for the two-minute drill. Remember this absolute truth, the perspective that we choose influences the perspective our child chooses. We must choose wisely. Let's don't repeat the mistake made by Adams' father.

The two-minute drill heightens perspective. The final outcome of the game depends on it because there are no "do overs." If we don't win, no one will remember us, or, at best, they will remember us as losers. As parents, we all want to win. We want to win our children's hearts, souls, minds, spirits, and their bodies. We want them to be quality people, filled with character, integrity, and honor. We can't wait until they are seven years old, or worse yet, teenagers, to start teaching these principles to them. We've all heard the theories that 85%of our child's characteristics are determined before their sixth birthday. I believe that to be true. At Big Oak Ranch, the younger we get a child, the better chance we have of molding them. As a parent, you may think that you have a span of 18 years to reach these goals. In reality, it's probably more like twelve years to fine-tune the foundation that you've already built prior to their sixth birthday.

As parents, we are here to lay a foundation in our child's heart that will enable him or her to grow into maturity. When we take away all of the parenting books in the world, all of the "experts," parenting is in its simplest form preparing our children for life. We can look at this quest as a privilege to develop our child's character, morals, values, and decision-making processes, or we can look at it as an impossible, insurmountable task. We also get to lead them to know Christ personally and make decisions regarding their eternal security, teach them how to choose a life mate, and teach them how to choose a life profession. In other words, we get to form a happy, well-balanced young adult who will choose a like-minded spouse. Talk about a ripple effect; if we produce a well-balanced adult and they marry a well-balanced adult, and they have well-balanced children, we have helped build a generation of productive individuals.

What Happens When?

As a parent preparing a child for the two-minute drill, we have different roles at different stages of the game. When a child is a newborn to six years old, the parent's job is to introduce them to the things they will need to incorporate into their lives. I believe some of the most important things we should introduce to them early are the Fruits of the Spirit as found in Galatians 5:22–23, "But the fruit of the Spirit is love, joy, peace, forbearance, kindness, goodness, faithfulness, gentleness and self-control."

We will never go wrong leaning on the real expert of child rearing, God Himself. He instructed us to develop the fruits of the spirit within our own lives. Why would that not be important for our children to know, as well? In the construction of any building, if the foundation isn't right, the building won't stand the test of time nor will it stand the blast of storms that will hit during its lifetime. The application to our children is obvious. The fruits of the spirit are the best foundation I know of that will enable any child to be all God intended them to be.

We need to teach them to find joy and peace where they are. They don't have to always have the latest video game equipment or toy to know joy. They don't have to constantly be "doing." It's important to teach them to do something as simple as sit by a fire they helped you build and cook a hot dog and then to find joy in that.

Kindness, goodness, faithfulness, and gentleness are what we teach our children to offer to others, and these attributes can't be faked. Our children constantly will look to see if we are kind, good, faithful, and gentle, and that the Fruits of the Spirit are real in our own lives! A marble temple can't be made out of mud and manure! We will reproduce what we are, be it a magnificent thoroughbred, a stubborn mule, or a busy Shetland pony who confuses activity over accomplishment.

We have to be openly honest and realistic about the attribute of our own self-control. Many adults lack self-control, and it is crucial in being a successful, well-functioning adult. We can't expect the same level of self-control from a young child. How many of us have had a young puppy that wasn't housebroken? You find that it has had an accident and as advised in so many books, you rub his nose in the "mess." Then you take a rolled-up newspaper and spank the puppy. Soon the puppy will realize what to do but we must remember a six-week old puppy can't control his bladder. It will be another two or three months, before he is able to do so.

No one wants a two-year-old running the household with his lack of self-control. We also don't want our own sixteen-year-old pitching a fit because he wasn't chosen as a starter in his sport or she wasn't chosen as homecoming queen. We expect this behavior from a baby who depends on us to be dry, clean, and fed. Our goal is to teach that baby self-control using common sense and setting reasonable expectations at each age.

It is a common thought in child rearing that children gain reasoning skills around the age of ten. Obviously some gain it at nine and there are some of us who think our children never get it. But the commonly accepted age that most believe reasoning skills are gained around age ten.

We must keep our expectations in line with their abilities to reason.

A Note to Single Parents

I've heard many times that air traffic controllers and other jobs of a similar nature are the hardest and toughest jobs in the world. That's simply not true. The hardest job in the world is being a single parent. If you are the single mom of a son, there is no way on your best day that you can know what it is like to be taunted in the locker room. Turning that statement around, no man will ever understand the physical and emotional aspects of a menstrual cycle. As a single parent, you must admit that you know what you know and excel in that area, but you've got to admit what you don't know and seek assistance with those things. That's the key.

As a single mom, there will be a time that you know what to do but that you might prefer to not do with your son, but you can rise to the occasion. What's wrong with you going fishing with your ten-year-old who has never been? Yes, it would probably be more enjoyable for him if a man taught him, but every great mom I know will do whatever it takes to help her son. If it means overcoming your disgust of putting worms on a hook, so be it. In reality, you can do most any-thing for your child.

For you single dads, when your daughter gets into a fight with her girlfriends, don't say, "Oh, nothing they said about you is true. Just get over it!" You've got to look your little girl in the eye and say, "Sweetheart, I don't know what it's like to have your three best friends' gang up on you and spread lies about you. I don't know what that feels like, but here's how I think you might consider handling it." Then, tell your daugh-ter what you think. But, you have to clarify the situation by admitting you don't know how it feels.

Do what you know you can do but don't pretend to know the stuff you don't know. Kids can spot you blowing smoke a mile away.

As a single parent, you have double duties, but your job is not impossible. You feel like you don't know what to do. That's OK! Admitting you don't have all of the answers is a sign of true wisdom! You can depend on God. He said, "I am the LORD, the God of all flesh; is anything too difficult for me?" (Jeremiah 32:27). In Numbers 11:23, God asked Moses, "Is the LORD'S power limited? Now you shall see whether My word will come true for you or not." Every night you need to ask God to give you the wisdom you must have to get through the coming day. Then, sleep soundly knowing and trusting He promised He will give you what you ask.

Stop and think about it for a minute. Doesn't it make sense that the God who gave you this son to raise wants you to raise him correctly? Realize when we pray and ask for God's guidance we are simply a child asking his dad for help. There's nothing wrong with admitting to God what He already knows: We can't do this. We need help. That's not disrespectful. That's a child asking his dad for help. Get up the next morning, learn from your earlier mistakes, and apply the lessons to the new day God has given. As already noted, only a fool keeps doing the same thing the wrong way and expecting different results. Admit where you messed up the day before. Ask Him to help you be a better single mom or dad than you were yesterday. Humbly admit that you can't do it alone. God is the ultimate gentleman. He will not force His way in, but He will come running when asked, as any loving father would. Ask Him!

All of us parents—not just single parents—will do well to admit that parenting is bigger than we are and ask God for help. His game plan is the wisest of all.

What You Can Expect If You Don't Train for the Two-Minute Drill

If we abandon our role as coach, our children will not be prepared for the two-minute drill of life when it comes. The Bible is very clear about some of the things we can expect to see in our children if we haven't prepared them. In 2 Timothy 3:1–4 it reads, "In the last days difficult times will come. For men will be lovers of self, lovers of money, boastful, arrogant, revilers, disobedient to parents, ungrateful, unholy, unloving, irreconcilable, malicious gossips, without self control, brutal, haters of good, treacherous, reckless, conceited, lovers of pleasure rather than lovers of God." Think about it. Is this what we want our children to become? If we do nothing to prepare, this will be the result.

Verse 5 continues, "Holding to a form of godliness, although they have denied its power; avoid such men as these." The word *form* means it's not the real thing. Anyone who holds to a form of godliness is not holding onto the real thing. Whatever they are holding on to will just be an imitation. Verse 7 continues, "Always learning but never coming to the knowledge of the truth." And then, in verse 9, "They will not make further progress, for their folly will become obvious to all."

To me, the scariest verse is verse13, "But evil men and imposters will proceed from bad to worse, deceiving and being deceived." If you don't build the foundation and get it right, there is going to be a slow deterioration, deceiving and being deceived, moving from bad to worse.

The Result

With Brodie, I didn't get it perfect. Just like all of us, he went through some bumpy times in his late teen-aged years and early twenties. However, the foundation was laid, and he became what we trained him to be, a fine young man. This happened only because we planned ahead and practiced for the two-minute drill.

"For the ways of a man are before the eyes of the LORD, and He watches all his paths." (Proverbs 5:21)

Chapter 2

M = Master

*The master you choose will directly affect
the master your child chooses.*

One day while Brodie and I were on our "transition" trip to Alaska, we were sitting and talking. "There can only be one master in your life," I told him. "There will be only one person in charge, one general, one captain of the ship. You get to choose who or what that master is going to be."

To illustrate the point, I took a knife out from my pocket and started whittling on a small piece of wood while we talked. I whittled a small rudder with a handle like you would see on most any small boat. That rudder was about an inch wide and was about one-eighth-inch thin. The handle was smaller but thicker and strong at the yoke where it connected to the rudder.

While I was whittling, I cut my thumb and bled on the handle. I kept working on it, and when I finished making the rudder, I handed it to Brodie and said, "When the entire world's falling apart around you and you don't know what to do, you're scared and alone, you're in trouble, look inside your heart. Ask yourself if you are sure you know who the master of your life really is. Then, I want you to pull out this bloodstained rudder and hold it in your hand. Let it remind you that you are the only boy on this earth who has my blood in him. That's who you are. You are mine. Remember that I believe in you, and that I know you will be a good man.

"However, most of all, I want you to realize that the hand of Jesus Christ is the One rudder of your life, and that He is the One guiding your ship. If you are living right, you might need to allow Him make a slight adjustment, allow a minor push on the handle to redirect the rudder. If you are not living right, you've got to get back on track. It will take a hard pull on that handle to make a major shift in where the rudder is taking your ship. That's how life works. You are going to have to constantly check to see who is guiding the ship, whose hand is on that handle."

I told Brodie he would not be able to serve more than one master. "No man can serve two masters, for either he will hate the one and love the other, or he will hold to one and despise the other. You cannot serve God and man" (Matthew 6:24). No person on earth can serve two things. Whatever we worship, we eventually serve. Whatever or whoever demands our attention will eventually become our god. It takes a constant check to see who or what is really in control.

Choosing a Master

The struggle of whom or what will be master of our lives is a daily one, especially for Christians. For most of us, it's the rebellious, selfish, arrogant, we-know-what's-best-for-our-lives attitude that we battle. It's a battle of who will be king of the hill.

Most adults remember king of the hill fights. As kids we would find a big mound of dirt like the ones found on construction site and stand around the hill. There would be one guy on top; he was king of the hill. The rest of us would then fight, claw, and scratch to knock him off of the hill. Once a kid knocked him off, that kid would be king of the hill until the next one came along and pushed him off. If you stop and think about it, every day is like that. There is only **one** spot at the top, and there are multitudes of people or opportunities just waiting to claim that spot as master of our lives.

I would love to tell you right now that Jesus Christ is the One who is always my Master. I could say that and it would read really well here in print, but it's not true. In that daily struggle, my ego can be the master; the ranch can be my master; the children who are here at the ranch can be my master; the mission and ministry I've been put on this earth to do can be my master; and my wife, children, and grandchildren can be my master. Many times, my own selfishness is my master. If you were to ask my children and grandchildren, at times they would probably tell you that they and my wife, Tee, are the most important things in the world to me. I kind of like them to think that Jesus Christ is my master, but I know the truth.

Not only does it matter who is guiding the rudder or standing on top of the hill, it matters how much of the day we allow that master to be in charge. The fruit of our lives is greatly determined by whomever or whatever is the master the majority of the time. We can't ask Jesus to be Master 10 minutes a day and then put ourselves in charge the other 23 hours and 50 minutes and expect His influence to make a great difference. The goal should be to turn our lives over to Him the entire day—all 24 hours—but none of us can, so our human nature is the stumbling block we all fight every day.

Children Know Who Our Master Is

The most tumultuous time for a child is when they start developing reasoning skills around the age of ten, and they start figuring things out. Some children come to this much younger, but for the most part, it happens around age ten. People ask me all of the time at what age do most people abandon their children at the ranch. It's around the age of twelve, and the reason is simple, you can't fool a twelve-year-old. A twelve-year-old knows what's most important, and they understand what's going on. They know that the alcohol you drink every night before dinner used to be just one glass and now it is four or five. Over a period of time, they have seen your dependence grow. They aren't stupid. Please understand that I'm not making a statement one way or another about alcohol. What I am saying is that children know when it or anything else becomes more important than anyone or anything else.

The ages of seven to twelve are tough years for children because everything is changing. The chemicals and hormones in a child's body bring about both physical and emotional changes. You, as their parent, are probably no longer the center of their world like you were for the first six years of their lives. At this point, their friends start taking over that spot.

Now that Tee and I are grandparents, we are reminded of the numerous couples we have talked with through the years who have told us they used to have a spend-the-night party for their grandchildren regularly. The grandchildren thought that their grandparents were their whole world. Then, something shifted when the grandchildren turned seven or eight. They no longer had as much time for their grandparents anymore. Activities and friends took their place. It wasn't something unusual. All children go through those changes. That's why from the time they are born until they are about six or seven, we have an opportunity to show them who our Master is, and to help them adopt and choose their own.

During the ages of seven to twelve, most children will reestablish and reaffirm who their master is, and, most likely, it will be the same master we have modeled for them, but then, outside negative influences hit. As they spend more and more time with friends, reality hits. They discover that other parents have other masters and some of them are going to be very scary and dangerous. Their eyes will be opened to outside influences. If a child's foundation isn't solid and strong, the temptation to join in the pursuit of other masters will be too strong. We can't choose our child's master; our child has to choose. However, you can model the very best choices for them, knowing that they will make some mistakes along the way. You won't win by judging, condemning, or blindly condoning their choices.

My own foundation as a child was a strong one. My parents taught me to withstand the poor choices that would come my way, but I didn't always handle those confrontations in the best way! I made one F as a student at the University of Alabama. This particular grade came in my freshman year. I was taking a basic science class with about 600 other students. One day the professor made the statement "It is only a very, very uninformed person who believes all the creation stuff, that there is One Supreme Being, and only one source of man."

I was just young enough and dumb enough to walk down to the professor in front of some friends and challenge him. I didn't do it for the friends, they just happened to be there. I looked at him and said, "It is a very narrow-minded person who doesn't believe that there is the possibility of another theory. I've also been told that it is a very foolish person who doesn't believe that there is an existence of another theory. I'm not calling you a narrow-minded fool, but if the shoe fits, wear it."

"There will be no need for you to come back to this class," he responded.

"I am not planning on coming back," I told him. So, I made an F in the class. In the scheme of things, I was stupid, but to this day, I don't regret my words. I could have been more tactful, less arrogant, and less confrontational. But I was sure of my foundation!

Where Does Family Fit?

If we are practicing believers, our families should have no doubt about whom our Master is, but should know that they are the next in line. Nothing or no one else can come before them. If a job or a possession takes priority over them, we need to seriously reevaluate. I've had the opportunity to make that decision more than most parents because of the privilege I've had to raise both my own two children and the more than 1,800 children who have called Big Oak Ranch their home. Let me tell you about one time, thankfully, that I made the right decision.

When Brodie was young, he and I were out working on my Jeep. That Jeep is the only real hobby I have. I had placed my tool pouch on the hood of the Jeep. Brodie wanted to help and reached up and pulled it off. It scratched the paint all the way across the hood. He immediately said, "Oh, no!" Quickly, I looked at him and said, "It's just a scratch. It's no big deal."

There have been plenty of times I didn't get it right, but in that moment when he thought he had really messed up I had the opportunity to let him know that he was more important to me than the Jeep. To this day, that Jeep has two scratches on the hood. You know what? They are priceless to me. Brodie is now a grown man, starting his own family. Those scratches remain a reminder to me, and hopefully to him, too, that he was and is more important than Daddy's Jeep.

What do we say to our children about the way we spend our time? Many years ago I started asking people this question: Name two things you did with your daddy that you'll never forget. I've gotten so many responses through the years. The responses have never related to a thing or to stuff. They always related to an experience. When I asked one friend to name the two things, his response blew me away. He shared with me that when he was eight years old, they had a father/son wild game dinner at his church. Among his group of friends, he was the only one whose dad took the time to attend the dinner with his son. However, on the flip side, he also told me about his hatred of deer hunting. He said that every Saturday morning in the fall and winter when they could have been watching football or deer hunting together, his dad went off with his own buddies to hunt. This man communicated to his little boy that he was important, yes, but that hunting with his own buddies was more important.

Another example of sending the wrong message might be a little closer to home. Are you the parent who arrives at school to pick up your child with your cell phone glued to your ear? These are the precious moments when your children may need to tell you about their day. Think of the child who made a 100 on his big test and couldn't wait to tell you, but your response was, "Just a minute, buddy, can't you see I'm on the phone?" Or, think of the day your child was chosen for the track team and was dying to tell you, but your higher priority phone conversation caused you to be too busy to listen to your child. We must be available to celebrate their successes with them. We also must be especially sensitive to them when they've had a tough day and need reinforcement and/or encouragement.

Because I'm stubborn like a mule, I sometimes have to learn things the hard way. One day when Brodie was around the age of four or five, he looked at me and said, "Dad, how come whenever I'm with you in the car, you are always on the phone?" Man. It changed my whole perspective in regard to my cell phone and my children in the car. Yes, there are times you have to be on the phone, but not all of the time. That phone call is not nearly as important as you spending quality time with your child. It's just a judgment and wisdom thing.

We must be careful that we don't waste our time on unimportant things when their needs and desires are so important. Life is full of disappointments, but when we can, in those daily, small moments show our child that he or she is the most important thing in the world to us after our Master and spouse.

My father worshipped the ground I walked on. My mom was even worse. I lost my only sibling, a younger sister, at an early age in a tragic accident. Losing her changed my parents' whole focus. Sometimes traumatic and tough things can alter and change who we put first. Sometimes, that change can be negative.

What about Work?

If you want to find out the honest truth about what's important in your life, ask a four-year-old. A four- or five-year-old doesn't have the ability to rationalize yet. They just see things as they are. What if someone asked your four- or five-year-old to name the most important thing in the world to you, what would your child name? A job? Exercise? Friends? Television? A hobby?

Even when you are working hard for good reasons, you may need to rethink how your efforts come across to your child. I remember a man who spent all of his time working very hard in his garden. To his child, the garden was the man's master. The child would have said that's where my daddy always is. He doesn't play or ever come in the house. But if you had asked the man about it, he would have said, "I'm raising food to feed my family. Times are hard. I love my family by providing for them." But you can't love your family, or profess your love for them, or even protect them, if you are an absentee parent. Children see things as they are, especially when they are between the ages of one to six. There are no filters and there is no cloudiness for them. They don't understand that your job allows you to provide for their physical needs. They just know when your job is your master. There's no fooling them.

Is Church Your Master?

If your church and your activities are your master, you've got it wrong. If church leadership is your master, again, you've got it wrong. Nowhere in the Bible does God tell us to sacrifice our families on the altar of ministry, there has to be balance. The Lord has to be first in our lives as Master, followed by spouse, children, and then ourselves and everyone and everything else. Those last two you can arrange any way we'd like.

Our children are looking closely at our lives and at how we live. They are not impressed because we serve in more church leadership positions than anyone else or that those responsibilities require meetings several nights a week. They are looking to see how we live our lives under the leadership and authority of the Master and how that impacts our life and theirs. They are looking to see that we have a healthy balance between meeting our responsibilities, like attending deacon's meetings, and being there for them.

How to Identify Your Master

During a child's early formative years, they watch every move we make. It says in Luke 6:40, "When fully taught, the student will become like the teacher." The student always watches the teacher more than the teacher watches the student. As we build character into a child, he or she is watching everything we do. They can tell who or what our master is, so, ask them! Evaluating ourselves is like looking at the back of our heads. We can look in a mirror to see our face but we need another mirror to see the back of our head. We can see our reflection, but we don't really "see" it. We are "guestimating" that our hair looks good or if we got a good haircut or if that bald spot looks as bad as we think it does.

Let's call them "blind spots." The best way to reveal the hidden blind spots is to ask those closest to us. Ask those who you know will tell the truth. Begin by assuring them you won't get angry with them because of their response and that you will not argue. If you are truly serious ask them to help you to see where you can do better.. Those closest to us see things we don't see. They may tell us that they see our master to be anger, money, exercise, or any number of other things.

Ask your children to identify your master. As I've said earlier, their perceptions are usually very accurate. If you have older and younger children, ask them both. You may even get different answers with their different views. If you get a common answer and it isn't the master you want for your life, you better know now that you are reproducing your mistakes in both of your children. They are already picking up on your wrong master.

If you really want to be the best parent and preparent for your children, then, please, don't get angry or defensive when a close friend or child tells you who they see to be your master and it isn't what you wanted to hear. You have a choice to respond or reject. Which one do you think will help you win? You can't learn, talk or think when you are angry.. You also have limited reasoning skills when you are angry. The Bible reads, "A gentle answer turns away wrath, but a harsh word stirs up anger" (Proverbs 15:1). It also reads, "A hot-tempered man stirs up strife, but the slow to anger calms a dispute" (Proverbs 15:18). And finally, "He who is slow to anger has great understanding, but he who is quick-tempered exalts folly. A tranquil heart is life to the body, but passion is rottenness to the bones" (Proverbs 14:29–30). If you continually lose your temper, you have validated your master isn't the Lord. Exercise wisdom in analyzing any information you receive, positive or negative.

We think we can fix everything in ourselves and others, but there are things that a mate, children, and best friends cannot see that only God can reveal. He can see down to the root of our problem. It may be that those closest to us see only the result of the root problem. Choose to get to the root instead of being a career pruner.

I believe that God wants us each to be a better version of who we already are. He wants us to be the best possible person we can be, not living beneath what we were designed to be. With His help, we'll get there. Here's how:

- acknowledge who God is
- confess the things that you know are wrong in your life
- thank Him for hearing you
- ask Him to show you where you are wrong
- Realize change is needed
- Be willing to change

God is going to answer that prayer! He promises in Psalm 84:11, "No good thing does He withhold from those who walk uprightly." God also says in His Word that He will honor those who honor Him. It is honoring to God when we ask Him to show us how to honor Him by correctly raising the child He gave us.

We were chosen by God Almighty to be our child's particular parent. Just think, in the whole universe, we have been chosen! He will also give us the plan to help us to be the best parent to that child possible.

Things To Do

1. Take a week and monitor your activities. Identify where you spend your time.

2. Ask your mate and children to tell you how they see you spending your time.

3. Look through your checkbook and determine what you spend the most money on.

4. After being honest with each of these, look back through what you've found and identify what appears to be the most important thing in your life. Be honest with your findings. Don't cheat at Solitaire!

5. Choose three people who will be honest with you. Talk with them about who your master is and who you want it to be. They can serve as a type of accountability council.

6. One late-night TV host makes lists of ten top things on a regular basis. Do the same. Write down the ten things that you think are most important in your life, not in any special order.

7. From that list, determine what you can change. You can't change that you have to work and your boss expects 40 hours a week from you, but you can change how you spend your time once you get home. Is TV your Master? Overeating? Working after hours? You can make adjustments to those things so that when you get home you can play pitch with your son, even if it means staying up later to do that work. I understand deadlines competing with the choice to play with your son. It's a choice worth making. Even to this day when Brodie comes home to visit, we will go out into the backyard and just pitch. We don't always talk. Those times are all the more special to me knowing that the average NFL quarterback throws 36,000 footballs in one season. 36,000! But when Brodie comes home, he chooses to spend time with me that way. It's a moment that was built long ago.

Summary

We have moved two houses onto the ranches—one to the girls' ranch and one to the boys' ranch. It was a fascinating process to watch, and I learned some interesting things. The mover explained to me that they would pick up the house and precisely measure the future foundation before they moved it. Then they would rebuild the footing and foundation on the new location exactly like it had been originally. Only then would they set the house down.

"The only way you will know that there is something unusual about the house is that above every doorframe, the sheetrock may crack," he said. "That will be the only way you'll ever know the house has been moved." He told me that it was just the way it is when a house is moved. As the house is set on its new foundation, above many of the doorframes, a crack will appear running up to the ceiling.

In your child's life, despite your best efforts to build the perfect foundation, there may be a few cosmetic cracks to appear above the doorframes. But just think about what will happen if you don't build the foundation correctly. You and your child are in for major cracks and problems. That's why it is crucial that you teach them to make regular checks on who or what their master is. It will help them avoid those cracks.

Brodie kept that rudder I whittled for him in Alaska in his billfold. Every time he opened that billfold, there was the rudder to remind him of my belief in him and to mentally check on whom or what was controlling his life at that moment.

One day, when he was in college, I got a call from him telling me he had lost his billfold. I told him not to worry. We'd alert the appropriate banks and so forth, and we'd get his cards and things replaced.

"No, Dad. I'm not worried about those," he said. "The rudder was in there." Of everything in his billfold, that was what he was most concerned about. That statement just reaffirmed for me that he had gotten it. All of the planning and practice from our playbook had been worth it. I replaced it with a different rudder the next time I saw him. It wasn't the bloodstained wooden one I had carved for him in Alaska, but I was proud to know that that one had served him well as a reminder all of those years.

"How blessed are the people whose God is the LORD!" (Psalm 144:15).

Chapter 3

A = Ask and Listen

Prayer is one of the greatest ways to lead, show, and tell our families we love them.

In the first two or three years of the ranch's existence, a friend came to see me and asked if I would help him with a matter at the local bank. He was a very good friend so I agreed. The president of the bank was also a good friend of mine. The three of us set up a meeting, and I introduced them to each other. The bank ended up giving a loan to my friend to start his business, a business that took off and flourished.

While the ranch was young and going through a financially tough time, there were days when we would have bills on the desk and no idea of how we were going to pay them. We had a small base of supporters we depended on, but we also knew that they were not the ultimate source of our provision.

On this particular day, we called the staff in, explained our financial dilemma and then joined together to ask God to help us. We had no idea where the funding would come from, but we knew God had called us to establish the ranch, and that He would provide for its needs.

God provided right on time, which is one of His greatest attributes. He shows up at the perfect time, every time. After praying and asking God to provide money to pay our bills, we walked out to the mailbox and found five $20 bills stacked together. Our unpaid bills totaled $98 and some change. Many of you reading this right now are saying, "Yeah, right." Well, let me finish the story.

Many years later, Brodie was playing ball with the friend I had introduced to the bank president and he looked at me and asked, "Did you ever find any money stacked in your mailbox?"

"We sure did," I told him.

"That was me repaying you for helping me get the loan to start my company by introducing me to the president of the bank," he said.

It wasn't until years had passed that we learned where those bills had come from. God did not physically place the five $20 bills in the mailbox, but God directed someone to put them there. I had no idea that the previous encounter would bear such fruit, nor did I know that it would impact my daughter to the extent that it did as she watched us simply ask God to help and provide.

Ask God

I believe modeling dependence on God is applicable to every family facing any kind of dilemma.

Call the entire family together that is age appropriate. Before sharing the details of any problems, tell them that as a family we're going to go to the Source of all help. We're going to the Author of solutions and the Guide through problems.

Of course, any details you share with your children should be age appropriate. None of us want our children to be terrified or up all night worrying. Imaginations can, and most times will, run rampant with bad news. But, think of the lifelong impression we can leave with our children and wives by reminding and reaffirming them that God has a plan for each of us and our families and then leading them to join us as we ask Him what His plan is in a particular situation.

It's so reassuring to know that God is a Father, too. He's not up in Heaven saying, "I hope you find My will." He's not hiding behind trees asking, "Have you found it yet?" Instead, He is sitting in front of us every day saying, "Please trust Me to get you through these tough days. I've got your back." He wants to teach us how to swim around the unseen boulders submerged just beneath the surface. He wants to teach us how to steer away from the whirlpools that would pull us under.

His help comes when we ask Him to guide us. Psalm 32:8 says, "For I will counsel you with my eye upon you and I will show you the way to go." We should commit this verse to memory if we want a baseline for handling tough times and seeking good advice for the direction we should go. Then we must show our children by our actions that not only do we trust the Lord with our lives, we show them and lead them through dark days with God's help because we know that the God that says He will counsel us and keep His eye on us is the same God that will meet our every need. He promised, and He cannot lie.

This approach will work for any family, regardless of its make-up of a traditional family or single-parent family.

I suggested to my friend that he begin praying

something like this with his family. "Dear God, I don't know what to do. The economy is flat. It looks like I might lose my job. I've got to take care of my family. I am asking You, my Lord and Savior, to show me the way through these dark waters."

Think about it. It's like going into a court of law with Wise Counsel rather than without it. I'm not calling God a Lawyer, but highlighting that same principle. Why should we go fight a fight if we're not prepared and we've not gotten wise counsel? He knows our enemy better than we do, as well as the outcome.

Imagine that right now we are looking at a massive mountain. God knows what's on the other side and the best way to get there. We're looking at it and deciding whether to try to climb over it, go around it, or dig under it. Our nature is to charge the mountain—straight up. I can only imagine God bending over the banisters of Heaven saying, "My child, the trail to the left was only 25 yards and it was flat. I could have gotten you around the mountain if you had asked for My help. Why did you take three days of exhausting effort to climb it? I would have had you around it in 10 minutes if you had just asked." If you flip that scenario around, sometimes we look for that easy way out and that quick little path that will allow us to avoid the climb, but then God says, "No, you need to climb over this one because there are lessons I want you to learn."

By asking for God's guidance and help, we show our families, especially our children, the Source of our strength and courage during tough days. They know who we *say* our Master is, but by asking for His help and then listening, we *show* them, and perhaps even ourselves, that He really is our Master. Remember, example outlives advice. We have to let go of that mind-set of thinking we know what to do. We must ask Him and believe in Him for guidance. I promise. He won't let you down, even when you don't think He heard you.

What a gift it is to our children to allow them to see up close how we face a dilemma, problem, or issue. By doing so, we give them the playbook by our actions, not our words. We can talk all we want and drag them to church, Bible studies, and church youth activities, but what speaks louder? Instead of telling them what to "do," we show them what we "are." I can promise you that years from now when our children are going through hard times and don't know where to turn, they will remember that on a consistent basis, we as parents said, "Lord, I don't know what to do," and then listened for His direction.

Listen

Listening is the most important part. Sometimes when we haven't asked for direction but we still hear a voice speak in our hearts, that's when it is especially important to listen. Let me give you an example.

When our daughter, Reagan, was playing women's basketball for the University of Alabama, the team was invited to participate in a tournament over a Thanksgiving weekend in Puerto Rico. Tee, Brodie and I went to support her. While there, we spent some time riding around and sightseeing. I turned our small rental car down this one particular road into a neighborhood. I should have paid a little more attention when I saw a pig eating trash on the side of the road, but I didn't pay attention or see the signs. I did notice that the street kept getting narrower and narrower and that there were cars parked on both sides of the road that made it difficult to navigate.

When the road got so narrow that we couldn't open the doors if we had wanted to, I glanced farther down the road to see a crowd of folks dancing, drinking, and having a party in the middle of the street. A voice spoke very clearly in my heart and said, *Get out.* I threw the car in reverse and backed out. I was so scared. When we got back to the top of that area, I was shaking and my hands were trembling. I said, "Dear God, thank You for protecting us." Brodie and Tee could see how shaken I was.

Back home I was talking with a friend who played on the Puerto Rican National Basketball team in the Olympics. He asked about our trip and I told him it was great except for this one experience in that one place. Before I could finish describing it, he stopped me and named exactly where we had been.

"You fool," he said. "The police won't even go down there. You could have been killed."

There we were tourists on a wrong road. Because I listened, we were protected. That's the point. That Voice in us that says *"Don't"* is something we should listen to. There have been lots of times when I've been ready to do something and heard the Voice, but stubbornly did it anyway. I can tell you this, with personal shame, because that's called rebelliousness or more plain and simple, sin. When you know that you are getting ready to do something wrong and still do it is rebellion. We won't ever go wrong listening to that Voice that says *"don't go there."*

Listening is not something that comes easily to most of us. We, in America, think that we have to talk all of the time. We think we're not in the conversation unless we're talking. We all know people who, when we're talking with them, aren't listening because their mouths are open ready to say what they're thinking.

All of the great men I know know how to listen. They don't spout off all of their wisdom. Their wisdom lies in listening. One of my dad's favorite things to do was to sit and listen to a conversation. He would say that by listening, he left with what he knew plus what the other guy knew. He figured he won every conversation because he left with more than the other guy did. It's simple, but true.

However, we all have to practice listening. Practice is the best way we can teach our children to listen. This is one skill that is learned by observation. Children learn from our examples and will pick up on it. But, we can only teach our children how to listen when we know how. I repeat we can't lead our families someplace we've never been or lead them someplace we're not going. We cannot teach our children how to listen to God if we're not listening to Him and to them.

Children listen with their eyes. We can preach and preach, but it will fall on deaf ears if they don't see us listening. There's a country song by Rodney Atkins entitled "Watching You" that describes it perfectly. In the song the little boy tells his dad that he wants to be just like him so he's been watching everything the dad does. That's the way it works.

As parents, it is easy to make a quick judgment about a situation without first listening and getting all of the facts. A well-intentioned mom found her six-year-old son dangerously close to the road and immediately began ranting and yelling about how dangerous it was to be there.

"All it takes is one slip or step and you could die," she yelled. "I can't stand the thought of spending the rest of my life without you. You know better than go there. Now, I want to know why you ran on the side of the road."

The boy's reply brought a quick halt to the mom's tirade.

"Ben (his little brother) was running toward the road, and I wanted to make sure I got to him before he got hurt."

You see? The mom was so busy talking that she had to have her say before listening to her son's reason. There is usually another side to the story that we should know. Great wisdom is stopping to listen to that other side and then basing our decisions on the complete information. I have been guilty of not doing this so many times. Through the years I have made many 180-degree turns that changed the landscape of my decision when I heard the other side of the story.

It's also important to remember that we can't be a giraffe and talk with or listen to sheep. We have to take on a sheep's heart to listen to another sheep. We are the adults, but we may be talking with a five-year-old boy who thinks he has discovered a creek that no one in the world before him has ever seen. Or, his heart has been broken because a little girl called him a name in front of his friends. Stop and remember what that was like. If it's an experience we've never had, we have to ask God for wisdom to be sensitive to it.

My heart still hurts when I remember the time Brodie was a young boy trying to tell me something. I looked off to the side, distracted. He put his hands around my face and pulled my chin around and said, "Daddy, I'm right here." That was a killer, and I've never forgotten that lesson.

Distraction impedes listening, so, I ask, what has you distracted? I can promise you that your children know, but the question is, do you? We get blinded to those areas in life where we fail, however, if our children see that we don't listen, we shouldn't be surprised when they don't listen.

One of the greatest weapons Satan uses against us is distraction, and I mean distraction in many ways. A good friend of mine shared this negative sequence about the road that starts with distraction. Distraction is the first stage in what we could call the "Six Stages of Getting Off Course."

First, we are distracted, then deceived, then defeated, then discouraged, then disillusioned, and then we hit despair. If we aren't living correctly and focused on our Master, then our children will see us in one of these six stages.

Stop right now and ask God to clear your mind, your spirit, and your soul. Focus on Him as the One who has given you your children. If you can't make it 60 seconds, you have to stop and ask yourself why? What distracted you? Children see and can pinpoint the distractions, be it money, power, improper relationships, the worship of sports, TV. You may think they don't know, but they do.

Identify where you may be in one of these six stages and what your distractions are. Don't wait until you hit despair before you stop yourself and learn to listen. It's like a corkscrew going downward. You start at the top and everything's good, but then in just one revolution, you are at deceived. Stop that downward rotation by practicing listening and applying.

Another exercise you may want to try is praying without asking God for anything. Just spend time thanking Him for whom and what He is to you. Allow your children to hear you. They will remember your words and prayers.

From the time I was a little boy, every Sunday a deacon in our church would stand up and pray, "Dear Lord, bless the sick and especially the sin sick." Fifty years later I went back to that church for a meeting, and they asked the same man to pray. His words were identical to what I remembered from my childhood. Now, I appreciate consistency when it's needed, but that prayer, to me, showed no sign of growth.

His walk with God appeared not to have changed because his conversation did not. My guess is that his listening skills had not changed either.

Men, we must also admit that women are better listeners than we are. We have to work at listening to our mates and children. It's easy for us to listen to our bosses explain how a project should be completed. So, we can listen. We simply choose not to listen other times—to our families and to God. Listening is truly an act of the will. We have to choose to, after a demanding day at work, listen without distraction to our mates and children. We have to choose to be quiet and listen to God.

Many times I will be driving down the road and turn off the radio and simply say, "God, I'm a mess. I don't know what to do. I'm so messed up inside. I'm thinking wrong things. I'm going in the wrong direction. I'm driving to this meeting to speak, and I've done it so many times before that it is just routine repetition. My mouth is like a tape recorder. I know that I can't function like this and be a useful tool in Your toolbox." Then I listen. Listening is acknowledging that we are tools in God's toolbox waiting for the Master to call each of us to fulfill our particular responsibility. We sometimes think we are in charge of the toolbox, but we're not.

Knowing When and How to Listen

My wife, Tee, and I have been married almost four decades. She still asks me at what point in our lives will I realize that she isn't interested in answering ten questions before breakfast. I'm just the opposite, I wake up and my motor's running in about ten seconds, certainly by the time my feet hit the floor. As children, both Brodie and Reagan were more like Tee, they all hated me in the mornings because I would go running down the hall and jump on their beds like the Energizer® bunny or, even worse, Tigger from *Winnie the Pooh*. That's how I woke them in the mornings.

Think about your child and when he or she is most talkative. If your child is not a morning person, you can't make the best conversation happen then. You can't, it just won't work. I got away with waking my children, but I knew that it was not the time for serious conversations. We have to use wisdom in deciding when and how to listen.

I find that time spent in the car with children is one of the best opportunities for meaningful conversations. Radios and in-car movies have stolen those moments of families talking with and listening to one another. I understand if you're driving 10 to 12 hours to Disney World you might not want to talk the whole way. Watch a couple of movies, then turn it off, and take a breath. Ask what everyone wants to do first when you get there. Then listen. Start mapping out your plan. It's like being a CEO of a company. Listen to the different divisions, and then pull them together.

The more we listen to our children, and they know that we are listening, the more they'll want to talk. One of the best ways to get them to talk is to ask questions, and not yes or no questions. Don't ask, "Do you like Mrs. Jones?" Instead, ask, "Why do you like Mrs. Jones?" or "What makes Mrs. Jones a better teacher?" Get them talking, and when you get an "I don't know," you should probably back off or redirect to something that interests them. We might be banging on a door that's partially closed but if you keep banging on it, it will close completely. Use wisdom and don't dig for those things that are tucked away in their chests. We have to let them hand those gems to us. When we listen to God, He will give us the wisdom to listen to them better, to hear what's being said, and more importantly, to hear what's not being said.

If we learn to listen to our children, they will tell us about their frustrations. When they talk about how they can't run as fast or jump as high as a friend, listen. When your daughter shares that she thinks her friend has beautiful hair and that she has ratty, curly hair, listen. Don't fall into the trap of immediately responding with things like, "People spend lots of money to have curly hair like yours." Just hush and listen to what she feels.

As parents, we also have to remember that not every conversation has to be "heavy." I am guilty of doing that with Brodie. One of the few times I've been totally crushed involved me trying to push a heavy conversation on him. He was home from college and we were at a hunting lodge getting ready to go out into the woods. I started talking with him about something and he looked at me with his eyes filled with tears.

"Dad, do you ever wonder why I always bring someone home with me on the weekends?" he asked. "Because every time it's just the two of us together, you always want to talk about something heavy."

It was a spiritual kick in the groin. *You idiot,* I said to myself. I still shudder to think about it to this day. From that day forward, I would work in a "heavy" every now and then, but was careful about when and how often. Before we discussed heavy topics, I would work in light conversation. Not that we as parents quit talking about the important stuff, but we have to pick and choose our battles, pick and choose the times to make something important. No child wants every morning's ride to school to be a heavy conversation. I learned from my son's wisdom that day to not make every conversation a heavy one.

Now, I may just glance at him and with one phrase say or ask something like, "Are you praying about your decisions? I know it's hard and want you to know I've got your back." With a statement like this, what have I told my child? It's your decision, but don't forget that if you need someone to talk with, I'm here. I encourage you to try this approach. You'll be amazed at how a statement like this will lead to more conversations.

As those conversations begin, really listening allows us to identify our child's true heart's desire. Knowing that our child knows how to listen to the Master and having a sense of the child's heart's desire is reassuring to us as parents when they start making those life decisions.

Things to Do

1. There's a country song about a man who describes his son as talking to God like God is a friend. Teach your child to pray by explaining that he or she can talk to God as a friend. A child will learn this by listening to you and your example.

2. As a family, thank God for every meal. We, as parents, can lead this with the simplicity of, "Dear Lord, thank You for the food You've given us as nourishment." As your child grows older, invite him or her to lead the prayer. You'll be surprised at the depth of the prayers.

3. Children pray innocently and without motive, and I know God loves this. Encourage your child's innocent, selfless prayers. Learn from them by praying

aloud with them without asking for anything. Simply focus on acknowledging who and what God is and expressing a grateful heart.

4. Make a conscious effort to pray when times are good. It's easy to pray when things are tough, but having a grateful heart when times are good takes practice.

Learning to Listen Is Good Preparation

During Brodie's senior year in high school, he was courted by several colleges to come to their schools and play football for them. There was a lot of pressure to go to Alabama, but Brodie's an independent guy and was just as open to go to Oklahoma, Miami, Florida State, or LSU. Those were the top five that we visited.

All along the process, I would ask him, "Are you praying about your decision?"

"Yes, sir," he'd say.

"What are you thinking?" I'd ask.

"Don't know yet," he'd respond.

I never rushed or pushed him. It had to be his decision. Here was a seventeen-year-old boy making one of the top five decisions of his lifetime. People would ask me, "Why don't you just tell him what to do?"

"I've raised him to be a man and to make his own decisions," was always my response.

At the very end of the process, we met Bobby Bowden who was the head coach of FSU at the time and Mark Richt, who was the FSU's offensive coordinator and the quarterback coach. They are great men and we have a very high respect both for them.

Mark Richt was at our house when Brodie finally said, "If you'll have me, I'm going to come to Florida State."

"Great!" Richt said.

Brodie called Bobby Bowden and said, "I'm your quarterback. Let's go." Everything was all set. The next day we were to have a press conference at Westbrook High School to make the announcement. We expected about 1,000 people to be there, including media reps from all over the country. It was a big deal because, at the time, Brodie was one of the top quarterbacks in the country.

I made Brodie call the other coaches from the colleges on his top 5 list after he talked with Bobby Bowden to tell them his decision. That was part of his responsibility.

Mark Richt left our house that evening and everything was finally settled. The pressure was off and Brodie was more relaxed than I had seen him in months. Unless you've been there, you just can't imagine the pressure athletes go through choosing a college. Going from college to the pros is a whole different animal because you get chosen, or drafted. From high school to college, it's just recruitment. The player makes the decision.

Later that night, after Brodie had left to tell his friends he was going to FSU, we learned that Mark Richt was leaving FSU and going to be the head coach at Georgia. Everything immediately changed. Brodie loved Coach Richt and respected him in every area, as a man, coach, father, and husband. A new decision had to be made and the pressure was back.

I called Brodie and said, "Bud, there's a problem." We decided to meet at a local restaurant to talk it through. When Tee and I got there, our daughter, Reagan, had beat us and was hugging and holding her brother. They have a really deep bond and love each other deeply.

The pressure was back and Brodie asked, "What am I going to do?" It was still his decision. I couldn't make it for him. It was time again for him to ask his heavenly Father and listen.

Brodie decided to speak to Coach Franchione at Alabama. I asked him over and over if he was sure. Alabama at the time had some serious issues with NCAA investigations (mistakes coaches had previously made) and the hammer was getting ready to drop. We just didn't know how hard it would be.

We met Coach Franchione the next morning in his office. Brodie asked him several questions. Then he said, "I'd like to come to Alabama." That was the end of it, and he walked out. The press conference went on that afternoon as planned, Brodie just made an announcement different from the one we had anticipated twelve hours earlier.

Looking back on Brodie's time at Alabama I can see how it made him a tougher, stronger man. Alabama didn't play for a national championship, they had recruitment issues, they got penalized, and they were placed on probation. He and the other players at Alabama were punished for the poor judgment of adults. Brodie asked me, "I was in middle school when this went down. Why am I being punished for something that happened years ago?" All of those things helped make Brodie what he is today. God knew it was best for Brodie, and Brodie had to depend on Him to get through that tough time. Asking God and then listening was part of Brodie's training. He was ready when the two-minute drill came and when it was time to make that life-changing decision.

The best way we can be great leaders in our families is to be followers of the Lord. If we get that right, we'll be great leaders. Ask Him and listen. If we get it reversed and listen to well-meaning, but incorrect sources, we becoming guilty of trying to lead God where we think we need to go. If we don't ask Him and listen, we and our children end up in trouble.

"For wisdom will enter your heart, and knowledge will be pleasant to your soul; discretion will guard you, understanding will watch over you, to deliver you from the way of evil." (Proverbs 2:10–12)

Chapter 4

N = Never Compromise

Compromise is not worth the price
you will pay to achieve it.

D ad, do you obey the law?" The question came from
Brodie in the car one day when he was about four years
old.

"Of course I do, Brodie," I said. "You have to."

"Then why do you have that machine on the dashboard
that tells you where the policemen are?" he asked. "Why
would it matter if you always obey the law?"

We got home, and with trembling hands I grabbed my
$300 "fuzz" buster and threw it in the trashcan. I never used
one again. I would love to say I've never sped again, but regret
to admit there are a few tickets that would disprove that statement. However, I realized that day that having that machine
in the car flaunted to my son that as long as the driver knows
where the policemen are, it's okay to speed everywhere else. I
never wanted my son to see me compromise again.

Compromise or Flexibility?

We all make choices every day in the different things that we do. In those choices, we can be flexible, or we can compromise. They look a lot like each other, but they are very different. Flexibility involves being willing to adapt and yield to the point of bending. It doesn't ask for a complete break. Compromise is a willingness to move from a principle to a middle ground, making a complete break. It involves conceding, and to me, conceding means losing. You have to give up on something you believe in and know to be true. The summer I was eight years old I learned that compromising something I knew to be true could be a matter of life and death.

As I previously mentioned, when I was five years old, my only sibling, a younger sister, died in a tragic accident. Both my mom and dad worked, which meant that I was a true latch-key child. During the school year, I would come home and either play ball with others or play alone until they got home from work. Summers were even lonelier because I had the whole day to myself—except for the summer when I was about seven or eight. I was so excited because that summer my parents agreed to let me attend a YMCA camp with some friends.

On the first day, the camp counselors announced that kids who could swim should go over to this group and kids who couldn't needed to go to the other group. I wanted to be with all of my friends, so I followed them to the group of swimmers. Now, I didn't know how to swim a lick, but that didn't matter. I was going to be with my friends.

The counselors were wise enough to not take our words for it. To make sure we could swim, they announced that even though we said we could swim, we would have to pass a swim test. They told us to line up in the lake and to swim from the bank to a certain point and back. Well, I joined the swimming group and made sure to stay up close to the bank. I started "swimming." Nobody but me knew that all I was doing was walking along the bottom, pushing along with my feet. I paddled with my arms and moved my head like I was supposed to, but my feet were firmly walking on the ground beneath the surface giving the appearance of swimming. I knew what I was doing.

Eventually, they said, "Okay, you've all passed," and told us we could head on out to the floating pier in the middle of the lake. As it always happens with any compromise, I got busted. As I headed out to the pier, obviously, the ground disappeared, and I went to the bottom. I pushed back up and poked my head above the water. I was pushing and trying to stay with my friends, but I had compromised the truth and ended up somewhere I shouldn't have been. I went down again and pushed up. The next time I went down, there was no bottom. It had just disappeared. I was under water frantically screaming, knowing I was about to drown. I finally found the bottom one last time and pushed myself back up. Just as my head poked up through the water, I felt a counselor grab the hair on the back of my head. He pulled me out of the water and into a canoe and carried me back to shore. I nearly died because I chose to compromise.

Another illustration of compromise is a simple one we can all understand since we've probably each done it at least once. Imagine driving down the interstate and taking the wrong exit. It's just a simple mistake. However, it becomes a compromise when we choose to stay on that exit and leave the interstate. We are going to get off track going the wrong way at some time or another. That's understandable and a basic human nature. However, we move into compromise when we know we've taken the wrong exit and then try to convince everybody in the car that we know where we are going. Everybody knows we've taken the wrong turn. It's pretty obvious, but we are numb to the truth and continue the wrong way. Staying on the wrong path is costly. We must be willing to immediately admit that we've taken the wrong exit and get back on the interstate. If we don't, we run the risk of becoming comfortable there.

The Comfort of Compromise

Compromise has a way of eventually becoming comfortable to all of us—both to you and to me. It's something we all battle every day. But, when that compromise doesn't bother us anymore, it becomes a way of life. At that point, we are in real trouble, especially when it involves our roles as parents. When we know a behavior or character trait isn't best, yet we let it keep going on, we are compromising and possibly setting up our children for disastrous consequences. We aren't training our child to be ready for life if we allow that five-year-old child to pitch a fit when challenged or told no. It's even worse when we allow a teenage child to do things such as be disrespectful to our spouse, be sarcastic to others, insult or put down others, or engage in behavior that we know to be questionable. Has it become more comfortable to let the behavior go rather than deal with it? I know that in your mind's eye you have already seen things flash up on your internal parent screen. The issue now is not, "Oh, I have failed as a parent." The issue is, "I have compromised. How can I fix it?"

One of the greatest ways to remove the comfortableness of compromise from our lives is to admit that it is a false comfort and then to become consistent in the way we handle it. Deep inside, when we compromise in our roles as parents, we know it's not right. Remember the interstate exit illustration? We don't say, "Oh, no!" and jerk the wheel to the left and go bouncing off the culverts, hills, and trees to get back onto the road. We got off gradually, and sometimes we have to get back on gradually. We need to get back on as quickly as we can, but we can't jerk the wheel and overcompensate. That's when we'll wreck.

How do we fix the teenager who is continually disrespectful? We sit down, talk, and let them know we are going to start tightening the screws. We must start by letting the child know that we know we have been wrong in letting it go and we will no longer tolerate that compromise of disrespect. We've learned and they must too, however, remember that they've been allowed fourteen or so years of being disrespectful, so we as parents can't come in with a cannon and blow their heads off the first time we hear it come out again. Habits begin gradually and most times have to be gradually broken, but it is imperative to begin.

Compromise isn't a once-and-done deal; it always brings with it a ripple effect of results. None of us want to compromise to the point that our children end up facing jail, an unwanted pregnancy, or in the extreme case, death, because we didn't set those boundaries and stick to them. If we keep hearing rumors about our children engaging in some activity or behavior that goes against what we know to be good and right, we have to deal with it. Perhaps the child is adamant that he or she is not involved. Just remember, most of the time where there's smoke, there's fire. None of us want to get the phone call at 2 a.m. asking us to come to the police station or to the emergency room. After raising over 1,800 kids at the ranch, I have been called to the morgue to identify a child's body, and I never want to have to do that again. We as parents can't get angry with our child because we had a good idea all along that that child was involved in something questionable but we chose not to deal with it. We chose the short-term comfort of compromise.

Common Areas of Compromise for Parents

The areas of compromise that we face as parents aren't unique or unusual. There are many that are common to us all:

Roles

One time Brodie and I were sitting around talking and he looked at me and said, "Well, Dude, what do you think?" "Whoa! Whoa! Time out," I said. "I'm not your dude. I'm not your buddy. I'm your dad. Don't you ever call me Dude again," and he never did. I know some parents who would think that it's cool that they are such good friends with their children and that they call each other by their first names or names such as Dude. Between a parent and child, there is a respect boundary that does not need to be waivered or breeched. We should never compromise our role as a parent to be a best friend, buddy, or Dude.

Respect

Let's go back to the simplicity of "Yes, Sir," "No, Sir," "Yes, Ma'am," "No, Ma'am," "Thank you," and "Please." If we allow our children to skip those simple addresses of respect, we do them a disservice. Sure, ignoring it and moving on would be easier. Doing it the hard way, but in a way that will better prepare them for life is to say, "If you talk to your mama like that again, then you are going to park your car for a week. I will not allow you to disrespect your mother. Remember, smart mouth and you lose your car, control your mouth and you keep your car. It's up to you." Then, you have to follow through.

We have to be good examples to our children. One of the saddest things I've seen through the years is the wife who talks to her husband like a dog, but talks to everybody else in a kind, sweet way. Then you have the husband who is verbally abusive to his wife, but talks to the family pet with more respect. The child in this situation grows up thinking that it's normal for a spouse to speak this way. Parents who are disrespectful to each other and then hold their children accountable for being respectful send a mixed message. The child will follow the example, not the words.

Work

The economy in recent years has been difficult, yes, and who knows when our country will really come out of it. But, that can't be our focus. Times are hard; people are losing jobs and not finding replacements. Those of us who have jobs are working harder than ever to keep them. Do we bring that work home with us? It is easy to justify a compromise on our family time because work demands it. Yet, we cannot afford to get caught in that trap. Who of us wants our children afraid to interrupt our time on the computer in the evening because we have work to get done? They have to know that they are the priority in our lives, and we have to live like they are.

What about our expectations of our children's work? Once we give them a job to complete, do we require them to complete it and complete it well? Allowing a child to get by or ignore their chores will teach them it is okay to work at that level. They will erroneously think it is okay on future job opportunities. If you look down the road, it is easy to see how this type of attitude will help them lose jobs, not keep them, all because we as parents failed to teach a good work ethic. The acceptance of mediocrity is the mortal enemy of excellence.

Time

We need to stop and ask ourselves "Are we too busy?" Does the schedule run us or do we run the schedule? Yes, there are appointments to keep and practices to attend and homework to be done. But, there has to be that sacred quality family time. Ask yourself, "When was the last time our family sat down at dinner and had a great meal and then just stayed there and talked?"

One of our favorite family activities is when Brodie, Reagan, and their families come to our house. We'll sit and eat, and then we clear the table and literally just talk and laugh for an hour or more. Those are the moments that are priceless. You're relaxed, your belly is full, and everybody loves on each other. We make fun of whoever ate four helpings of banana pudding, all the while saying, "I really shouldn't."

It's in those times that building relationships happen. We've gotten so busy that our relationships suffer. The only time many husbands and wives talk is on the phone on the way to the next event. I admit with shame that there are times when I'll be coming home from a trip and meet Tee at a ballgame or something. As we head home, we'll talk for the first time in the day and it's already 9 o'clock at night. It happens to us all, but we should work to make it happen less and less, not more.

We have conditioned ourselves to believe that compromising quality time with our spouses and the family is okay. We cannot allow ourselves to be guilty of confusing activity with accomplishment. We think the busier we look, the better the parents we are. How many times have you been asked, "How are you?" to which you reply, "Oh, I just got back from (fill in the blank) and I have to be at the next thing at 3:30. I'm not going to have time to get a meal together so I'll pick up some takeout on the way home. This will be the eighth night in the row we've done that, but we're just so busy right now with (fill in the blanks)." Or, "Man, things are really crazy at work right now. We have that project due next week and it has meant late nights and some out-of-town trips. I haven't seen my kids in the last two weeks except for a few hours the last two Sunday mornings, but that's what we have to do to get work these days."

We must be brutally honest with ourselves about time management. It can become a negative god or a useful ally in building great relationships with our families. When friends and family ask, "How are you doing?" how often do we respond with the laundry list of all that we are doing and secretly get a little adrenalin rush from it? Stop and recognize it. Call it for what it is. The question wasn't "What are you doing?" It was "How are you doing?" I was just with a small group of friends when one of them came over and put his hand on my shoulder and asked, "How are you?" He wasn't interested in all that I was doing. He wanted to know how I was doing. That's a friend.

If we don't know our child's five best friends, we are too busy. We all need to invest time in meaningful conversations with our children and their friends. I'm not talking about giving sermons, but really listening to them. I promise you will be amazed at what you will learn, especially about your own child.

Replacing Electronics for Relationships

We've become electronic families. Recently I was in a restaurant talking with a couple when the mom said, "Just a minute," and then texted their daughter who was three tables over with friends. They couldn't get away from texting for that one moment. The mother was emotionally tethered to the daughter, but I can assure you the daughter wasn't emotionally tethered to the mother.

Worth

So many parents draw energy, or worth, from their children. Foremost, we are to draw our worth from God. Drawing worth from our children is unhealthy and unwise. We can be proud of who and what our children become but should not draw worth from them. I admit that I am one of the proudest parents you will ever meet. I would put Brodie and Reagan up against any man or woman any day because of the great mom my wife has been to them. They are now young adults but still call her and ask her opinion. What an awesome gift for our children to seek advice, but not worth from us, just as it is true that it's an awesome gift to them that we not depend on them for our worth.

Pride

I've said before that I believe the most difficult job on this earth is being a single parent. If you are raising a child of the opposite sex, there is no way you can fully know what they are going through as they mature. Moms can't know what it's like to hurt as a boy. I'm not saying that males hurt worse or less, we just hurt differently. The same is true for a dad raising a daughter. Single parents set themselves up to fail because of pride and ego when they say, "I can handle this," when in reality you can't. Please be willing to ask a trusted brother, sister, uncle, aunt or friend to help you over the hurdle.

Wisdom

The Bible is very clear that if we ask for wisdom, it will be given abundantly. "Now if any of you lacks wisdom, he should ask God, who gives to all generously and without criticizing, and it will be given to him" (James 1:5). Why would we compromise and settle for anything less? Trust Him. I have lost every time I didn't.

Our Children See and Learn from Us

Clearly, compromise is never forgotten, not by me in that near-drowning experience or by our children as they watch us. We hear compromises all day long and many times it doesn't register as such. We live in a visual world and the things we see are burned into our minds. Those compromises stick with us.

I met a little boy who showed me his back where his dad had beaten him for smoking marijuana.

"What happened?" I asked.

"I smarted off to my dad," was his reply.

"What did you say?" I asked trying to imagine what would provoke a dad to do such a horrendous thing.

"Well, my dad was getting ready to beat me, and I said, 'Dad, I smoke my dope and you drink yours. What's the difference?'" he told me.

That dad was trying to live under a double standard and his son nailed him. Leaders can't live under a double standard.

I've heard a story about a child who came in with a zero on his schoolwork and of course the dad went nuts when the boy admitted that he was cheating.

"You were cheating?" the dad raged. "Where did you learn to do such a thing?"

"I watched you do your income taxes last month and you were talking about ways to cheat the government by not declaring different things. I thought that if it was okay for you to do on taxes, I could do it on schoolwork."

For you moms, how many of times have you answered the phone and told the caller that your husband wasn't at home when he was sitting right there, but choosing not to take the call? You can't lie in front of your child and then scream at her when she lies. If you practice lies your child will grow up thinking that lying is okay.

Think about the dad who is up watching TV after everyone else in the family has gone to bed. He's flipping through the channels and something inappropriate comes on. He sees it and moves on. That's resisting temptation and it is not sin but when he intentionally turns the channel back to it, that's compromise and is a sin. What if the dad hears a bump at the end of the sofa and discovers his ten-year-old son has been sitting there the whole time without him knowing it. He thought that his compromise was unseen, but now the son has been exposed to sin.

There is always a set of eyes nearby. For those of us who are Christians, obviously, it's the Holy Spirit in us convicting us of what we know to be wrong. I truly believe in that the gut feeling or inner voice that says, "*Don't go there. Don't do this*" is the Holy Spirit. When we hear that voice and choose to go ahead, that's not only us compromising; it's an outright consequence decision to compromise. We're all guilty of it.

Never Compromise Discipline

We are our child's parent, not their best friend. God has given them to us to teach and train them to the point that they become adults who are responsible and prepared for their world. Our parents did that for us. Two generations ago, those parents did it for our parents. Many of their discipline methods differ from what we use today. For them, it was okay to take their hand and slap a child. We have learned that while that may work, it's not the best way to discipline at child. There are other ways to discipline them. In our family and on the ranch, we believe in spanking, but never beating. There are three levels in disciplining a child. Discipline trains and a child will always remember what it was for. Punishment is rarely effective or remembered, and sadly, abuse will never be forgotten.

There are concessions, not compromises, which we as parents must make when it comes to discipline. For example, a six-month-old who has not had anything to eat nor has a dirty diaper is going to cry. You have to feed and clean the baby, that's just common sense. A child between the ages of birth and two-years-old is in charge. Let's just admit it. They have to have help with every function of life. Our schedules, sleep patterns, and our time off revolve around the child. But, as they get older, those demands have to be identified for what they are, selfish demands. Teenagers will make similar demands and act like babies, but our job as parents is to have disciplined and trained them earlier in life so we can avoid those tantrums. Who of us hasn't heard of a teenager standing up to a parent and saying, "I don't care what you think, I'm still going to [fill in the blank]." No! The word *no* is a good word, and we should never concede or compromise that God-given right to train up a child in the way he or she should go. We are to never concede or compromise that right, that privilege, that honor, and that responsibility.

Recognizing Compromise in a Child

The teenage years bring with them lots of changes that are natural. Those changes may be trying and difficult to navigate as a parent, but they are normal. We need to worry when we see the norm or natural move to an unnatural level, such as drastic mood swings, drastic changes in behavior, a drastic increase in secrecy and hiding, and doors that are closed for abnormal extended periods of time.

There has to be a balance in everything. Teenagers will have those swings in mood and behavior, but when a happy-go-lucky, wonderfully joyful spirit becomes dark and empty, the eyes will give it away. At that point it is time to work hard and not just let it go. We shouldn't pass off our responsibility by saying, "Oh, it's just a phase they are going through." Yes, it is a phase, but wisdom will allow you to see the difference between that phase and compromising behavior. One of the hardest things about being a parent is discerning and knowing the right questions to ask and then being able to read between the lines of their answers. That ability is so important when dealing with a teenage child going through hormonal changes. Only wisdom from God allows us to see what needs to be seen. Ask Him. "But if any of you lacks wisdom, let him ask of God, who gives to all generously and without reproach, and it will be given to him," (James 1:5).

66

Things to Do

1. Look for opportunities to choose to not compromise. For example, when you have purchased an item and paid for it, if you are given too much change, return the overage and explain the situation to your child. It is a life lesson your child will never forget.
2. Let your child experience, see, and understand that your word is your bond. When you say you will do something, you do it. They should never see you compromise in your business dealings, your family dealings, or your personal dealings with your mate. Let them always see you choose integrity, no matter what.
3. You will lose your integrity if you say something like, "Pick up all of this wood, and then you can go fishing," and then don't require the child to follow through. If the child doesn't pick up all of the wood but you let him or her go fishing, you have compromised. There are times when you should be flexible, but there is never a time you should compromise. The "It's-OK-that-you-didn't-finish" syndrome is not acceptable. Our society has become lax in requiring that we finish the job, but as parents, we cannot.

Compromise Costs

As parents we have a choice to make when it comes to dealing with issues with our children. We can meet them head on or we can "run around the block." Anyone who has ever played football has heard the term and knows what it means when the coach says, "Don't run around the block." That's the easy way but not best way.

As two opposing football teams line up facing each other, each player has an assignment. For the offensive line, the assignment is to protect the quarterback. Defensive players line up facing the offensive players and have the exact opposite job. Their job is to, at all cost, get to the quarterback or whoever has the ball.

In every play, each defensive player has a choice. He can try to run through the "block" or around it. This means he must be willing to meet head-on the offensive player coming straight at him, or choose to avoid that head-on collision by choosing to run around the wrong side of the opposing player.

Some players who think they are really fast may choose an alternative route, but it almost never works. By the time the defensive player has run around the outside of the "block," the ball carrier will be down the field.

At that point, the defensive player is left with no other choice but to pursue. If he had chosen to meet the force head on and run through the block, he would have had a much better chance of stopping the ball carrier before he even moved down the field.

Running around the block is the equivalent of taking the easy way out and can cost yardage and points in a football game. In parenting, we have the same choice. We can choose to meet issues head on and have a better chance of dealing with them before they move or grow into something bigger, or we can choose to compromise and "run around the block." If we choose to "run around the block," we will end up pursuing or chasing the problem. It's our choice.

"Many are the plans in a man's heart, but the counsel of the Lord, it will stand." (Proverbs 19:21)

Chapter 5

H = Handle Your Business

*We work so hard to give our children the things
we didn't get growing up that we forget to give
them the things we did get.*

Several years ago we had a very wise housemother on the
Big Oak Boys' Ranch teach one of our kids a lesson about
work ethic that will last him a lifetime. Seven boys were getting ready one morning to go haul hay. Now hauling hay in
the summer is hard, nasty, sweaty work, but it's got to be done
if you're going to feed the animals during the winter.

"I'm not hauling hay," this one boy defiantly said that
morning.

The housemother said, "Okay, fine." She then told the
house dad, "I'll take care of this. You take the other boys and
go on."

The dad and the other boys left and spent the entire day
working hard by hauling hay. When they came back that

evening, they found that the other boy had just been at home relaxing and having a good time.

For supper that night, the housemother served steak. I don't know where she got them, but she had steak for every kid but that one boy. He didn't have a steak.

He sat there looking around and then indignantly said, "Where's mine?"

"What is steak?" she asked.

"It's beef," he replied.

"What do cows eat in the winter?" she asked, continuing the questioning.

"They eat hay," he said.

"Did you haul any hay today?" she asked.

"Well, no Ma'am," he said.

"Okay. You don't get to eat beef because, see, if you don't help feed them, you don't get to eat them," she replied.

The next morning, guess who was the first one up saying, "Guys, let's go. We have got to go get some hay for those cows."

That housemother took a simple tool and taught that boy a valuable lesson that was practical and impactful.

Three Keys to Success

We've been sending kids to college from the ranch since 1974. In all of them we've seen that three things will either be their downfall or will ensure their success. The first key is time management, the second key is money management, and the third key is work ethic. They are like a pyramid of success for an eighteen-year-old going off to college. They are also the keys to making it in life.

When I was a sophomore in college, Coach Bryant said,

"The meeting will start at 1:20." That didn't mean 1:21. My roommate came in 12 seconds late for the meeting. Coach Bryant asked the head manager, "What time is the start of this meeting?" The head manager said, "1:20, Coach." Coach Bryant looked at my roommate and then looked at the head manager and said, "Take his Auburn tickets."

Tickets to the Alabama/Auburn game were like gold. Because of 12 seconds, my roommate lost a lot of gold. What an impact that made on the rest of us. There was no doubt from that point forward that we were to manage our time correctly.

As our children go to college, we must ask if they have the same respect for time management. We can't let it go if they are always late. Think of it this way, there will be a professor who says, "The final exam is at 8 a.m. sharp." If you allowed your child to always be late, and it was okay to be a poor time manager, that doesn't mean the professor will overlook the tardiness for the exam by opening the locked door once the exam has started. It would be tough to have to accept a zero on an exam you never got to take!

We tell our children, "One day you will have to know how to manage your money because you'll only have X dollars a month coming in each week. You won't have a cash cow of an extra thousand a month. You will have to know how to manage and live on that X dollars."

As parents we need to teach our children how to balance their banking accounts and how to handle their debt card. There are some of you thinking, "Have you lost your ever-loving mind? Give my fifteen-year-old a debit card?" No, you aren't giving them a credit card. You are teaching them how to handle their finances. It's not a card that can be used just because it's in their wallet. Get a debt card that allows you to put funds into their account and will not allow them to exceed their limit. Give it to your child and clearly discuss exactly what that money should cover during the month. If, after the third week, your child runs out of money for gas because they blew it on two pounds of bubble gum or stopped for $6 worth of snacks every afternoon, you have an opportunity to teach them about money management.

Let's say the funds were to cover gas for the month. It will only take one time of running out of money and having to depend on you to take them back and forth to school, other school activities, picking them up from practice, or chauffeuring them around because they didn't manage their finances. If a school bus goes by your home and you say, "You ran out of money, you will need to get a ride on bus," it will only take one month to learn their lesson. It also will only take one time for your son to be embarrassed in front of a date or friends when he has insufficient funds on his debit card. There are lots of ways to teach the proper way to handle a credit or debit card. As a great parent, I know your mind is racing with different ways to teach them this lesson.

In today's society, work ethic is crucial. We're almost emasculating our boys because we're raising them to not know what a hard day's work is. They don't know what it's like to lie down at night, exhausted from hard, physical or mental work.

Tee and I put Brodie to work in the horse barn when he was 9 to clean out the stables. You may think that it was too young, but I don't think so. To this day, one of his greatest strengths is his work ethic. We do the same thing with the boys here at the ranch. I have breakfast with them every Tuesday morning at 7:00 o'clock and the high school boys ask me all of the time, "Why are you so hard on us?" Jokingly I tell them, "Because I love the girls more," but the real reason is I want them to be ready when they're 24 years old and they're tired from a hard week of work in which their boss has pushed them, and they're tired of being verbally, emotionally, physically, and mentally challenged. As they are tempted not to show up for work, they need to know that that decision may cost them the job. They would then have to come back the next day and look a wife and child in the eyes and say, "I'm sorry, Daddy got fired because he stayed home from work yesterday."

We push the boys to know that you get up in the morning whether you feel like it or not and go to work.

Enjoying the Fruits of Your Labor

I strongly encourage you not to give your child a car. Let them buy it for themselves. A lot of you are gasping, saying, "No!" There is nothing wrong with a child having an investment in the car they drive. In fact, everything is right about it. Anything freely given loses value. This is our practice at the ranch and we think it's very important that our children buy their own cars. We provide them work opportunities to earn the money and teach them how to save for that purchase. It's amazing how they take care of those cars more than kids who have been give one.

I've had this conversation with boys on the ranch many times. I ask them to imagine themselves at the age of twenty-one and they're sitting around talking with a bunch of their buddies and some girls when someone asks, "What kind of car do you drive?" One guy might say, "Well, my dad gave me a truck." Another, "My dad gave me a Mercedes." The third one might add, "Well, my dad gave me a Lexus." When they ask the boy from the ranch what he drives, he can respond, "Well, when I was fourteen or fifteen years old I worked all summer long and saved my money. When I was 16, I worked that summer, too. When I was almost 17, I was able to buy my own vehicle. The title has my name on it. It was mine. When I graduated from college, I traded that car in and bought a better car. It's paid for as well, completely debt-free, and that title has my name on it, too."

I tell the boys "Hear me clearly. Of the four girls sitting there, three might say, 'Wow! His dad gave him a Mercedes.' But there will be one or two girls that will look at you differently." I tell them that the fact that they are already thinking ahead will be attractive because so many boys at that age are just thinking about their next toys, their next rifle, their next skiing adventure, or their next boat.

Our boys learn early to think ahead about things such as how to afford a new boat or whatever. No one is going to give it to them. They will have to earn it. That work ethic will carry them a long way in life.

I finish my conversation by telling them, "Oh, yeah, and by the way, that girl that was attracted to you and impressed by you because she saw that you have a good work ethic, I guarantee she will be a good girl who will make a great wife and awesome mother to her children because she knows the value of that deep embedded strength that you have of being able to handle business, even at the age of sixteen."

Never Lie

When a child asks for a new bike and as a parent you agree to buy it together with them, paying for one-half and the child paying for the other half, you can't change the agreement. If the child is $50 short when it comes time to buy the bike, you can't suddenly say, "Well, I'll cover it. Don't worry about it." If you do, you are lying to that child. Plus, you won't be preparing him or her for later in their life.

What's going to happen when they are older and they're dealing with a banker or car dealer and they are financially short? That child will be "business crippled." They will be hit with the reality of "this man is not going to help me!" This is real life, and we must train our children for the realities of real life. Excuse me; I should say the brutalities of real life. If our children always expect that every time they go into a meeting the other guy is going to change the rules, we've set them up to fail. The other guy isn't going to change the rules. The banker has a set formula to go by as well as the real estate agent and every other individual in the business world. There are guidelines they can't change. We must teach this principle to our children, and we do that by always telling the truth and sticking to it.

There are times when flexibility is called for and in order to build a trust and belief factor with our children, there are times when we might want to say, "Okay, I'll pay the extra $20 but you will need to pay me back." But, be sure you always get that money back. We can't let it go because the child will think that it's going to happen for the rest of their lives. People are just going to let things go. It is the same reason so many drug addicts can never get off of drugs, family members continue to enable them. We must not allow them to get caught up in the "It's-Okay-Don't-Worry-About-It" cycle.

Work and Allowances

At the Big Oak Ranch, we expect and encourage our children to work and earn their own money. Here's how it works. Let's say a child earns $100 a week raking leaves, mowing grass, and washing cars. We tell him he must save 70 percent of it, tithe 10 percent, and the remaining 20 percent is money he can spend on whatever he wants to buy. If he wants to buy a special pair of cowboy boots, or a bow for hunting, he has to save for those things.

We also teach them to plan ahead. If there is a dance coming up and the boys have to wear tuxes, purchase tickets, flowers and even pay for dinner, we encourage them to plan far ahead. They know in January that they will have to have the money in April. That gives them several months to be ready for those expenses.

When the children leave the ranch to move out on their own, that 70 percent they saved is there for them to take with them. When a child has saved and scrimped and done without extras and watched others buying expensive soft drinks at Disney World, he will be reminded that he drank water from the water fountain. When that child is able to purchase a car, he will remember the true price he paid for it and understand that it is a privilege to purchase and own the car, not an entitlement.

We shouldn't give a child an allowance just because they are breathing. That's not right. We give the allowance in return for chores that help maintain, run, and operate the home. Allowances are not a free-gifted right just because they are members of the family. Allowances are funds that will help them learn how to deal with money. We can't fall into the trap of saying, "I'm not paying them to do chores." An allowance is an opportunity we can use in coaching them to handle finances correctly. If we don't, when they are eighteen and leave for college, they will walk into that freshman dorm, and we hand them money for food that should last a month. I guarantee they will crash and burn because they don't know how to handle their finances. If they didn't learn when they were six, seven, eight, or ten years old, they will be ill-equipped to be successful in life. An allowance trains them for the future.

Look even beyond college. Many divorces simply happen because two people didn't learn how to manage money and money became their problem, therefore the marriage exploded. It is a train wreck when there are two unprepared, ill-trained, and inexperienced money-handling partners in a marriage. Someone in the marriage must exercise financial wisdom. It's not fun to have to say things such as, "We can't go out and buy a new car simply because we saw one on a commercial and now we want it." Or, "You can't go out and buy a brand new dress simply because you want it." But, a financially wise person will respond by saying things like, "We can certainly talk about this purchase and make a plan to save toward it." Purchases made after planning and saving are always more appreciated.

Numerous times we've had children say, "Well, I don't think its right that y'all make me do all of these chores, and I just get an allowance. I think you should pay me." This is how we respond. "Okay, fine. We'll start paying you for that work, and then we'll also start charging you for the food you eat." A child will lose this argument every time.

If they want to operate in a business atmosphere, give them a real life business situation. I promise you it will quiet the comments like, "I don't think this is fair." They'll get the picture and understand.

A wise mom and dad will sit down and say, "Do you realize that right now your share of the power, water, mortgage, food, and health insurance is $800 a month? Right now your allowance is free and clear. Would you like for us to start paying you for your chores and then take out your portion of the monthly expenses from you allowance? We can do this any way you want." It's amazing how quickly they will do the math. They're not stupid. As parents, we also can't be stupid by letting them con us out of doing chores. Chores and a good work ethic are a must for any child to be successful.

What Age Is the Right Age?

At the Big Oak Ranch, we begin with teaching preschool children how to do chores. Obviously, we can't demand the same levels of chores from a two-year-old as we do a six-year-old. But, you know what? You can teach a two-year-old to pick up his toys when they are finished with them. It is not a good thing for us as parents to always clean up after them when they finish. We can help them, but should never do it for them. The child should have an investment in picking up their toys.

The same is true when "accidently," on purpose, a child knocks over a cup of milk just to see what happens. We can't scream, yell, get mad or come unglued because *we* are embarrassed. Instead, try, "Oops. You spilled your milk. *Let's* get some paper towels and clean it up." Guess what? They learn to be more careful instead of thinking they have a maid called "Mom" or "Dad" who runs to clean up every mess. Teenage children need to know this even more. Too many teens have this inappropriate safety net called entitlement.

At this early age, we can also begin creating a giver's heart in our children. Let's just face it; every child has a selfish streak. It is a built-in natural phenomenon. Wise parents, however, learn that they can train their child to have a giver's heart.

When Brodie was five and Reagan was nine, we took three little boys, who were brothers, into the ranch. One of them had been burned with cigarette butts around his stomach. I had given him a bath and when we came out from the bathroom, Brodie was standing there with all of his clothes in his hands, including his underwear and the GI Joe pajamas his mother had bought for him that day.

"You don't have any clothes, take mine," he told the little boy. He them dropped all of his clothes at the boy's feet. Reagan was standing behind him, and she stepped forward and said, "Come here, let's fix your wounds." They responded this way because of the example their mother had given and shared from her giver's heart. They had been trained to also be givers.

When Brodie was two he was selfish just like any other two-year-old. We can't expect any child, on their own, to respond unselfishly. Brodie and Reagan had learned that giving is a much better than taking. That kind of training takes consistent effort. We can't let our children be selfish one day and then the next day abuse them because they are selfish. And, to be perfectly candid, this training takes place from the time they are born until the time they leave for college.

By the way, those three boys lived at the ranch until they each graduated from high school. All three are now grown men and hold responsible jobs. The two oldest brothers work for a tree service company and the youngest works in construction.

Robert Fulghum wrote *Everything I Need to Know I Learned in Kindergarten* for humor, but to be quite honest, the title is accurate. It is estimated that 85 percent of a child's character is determined by the time he or she is six-years-old. None of us want to produce a selfish child. Therefore, training our children in the art of sharing with others at an early age is a must. It is a standard life lesson that we cannot let slip away because the older they get, the harder the lesson will be to teach.

There is a different dynamic at work in teaching children ages six through twelve to handle their business. Our living examples during these years will outlive anything we ever say. When our children are with us riding down the road and see a woman sitting on the side with two small children and a sign that says, "Homeless," they will remember if we stopped to give her food. Notice, I said food, not money. They will remember that we helped others, or they will remember hearing us say, "Get a job and quit being a beggar." We decide what we want them to learn from us.

A few years ago, I was visiting Brodie in Kansas City for a game between the Chiefs and the Green Bay Packers. After it was over, we were riding down the road, going back to his house. There was a man on the side of the road, and his clothes were tattered, holding a sign that said, "Homeless, need work, need food." Brodie had a big bag of beef jerky in his truck, so he rolled down the window and handed the guy the jerky before we drove away.

"He's probably going to sell it," I said.

"You know what," he replied, "I don't care what he does with it. My job was to give him something to eat."

Mentality, that is important. Yes, there are con men and women out there, but there are also people out there who really do need our help. It's not our role to judge because we don't know the rest of the story of the man in Kansas City or the woman with two children on the side of the road. It's our role to help. I am not condoning the extremes of saying go sell everything you have and give it to the poor. That's not what I'm suggesting we teach our children. There is balance in everything we're teaching our children. We must set a good example of sharing because there will be no "do overs" on this one.

How cool would it be to ride down the road and hear your son say, "Hey, Dad, can we help that guy? I'll give part of my allowance. Can we help him?" Or to hear your grown son say, "My job is to give him something to eat." That's what we're after, to get to that point where we as parents have to model good stewardship to them. What we do in front of them long outlives what we say.

Chores also give us a way to work with our children. No adult would ever ask a seven-year-old to drag a 100-pound bag of dirt from the car to the house; all we would do is create animosity and frustration. But how much better would it be to say, "Hey, Buddy, come here and help me get this wagon and that wheelbarrow. We're going to move some dirt." Let the seven-year-old stand between you and the loaded wheelbarrow, allowing him to help you lift and push that dirt. Together you can fill the hole in your yard and plant grass to cover the dirt. Ten years from now he'll say, "Man, I remember the day my dad and I fixed a hole in the yard. That was a great day because my dad needed me to help him." Opportunities like that will create a work ethic and strengthen your bond. That can't be found anywhere else. Trust me on this one.

With children between the ages of twelve and eighteen, obviously they can do more. We have to remember, though, that as the jobs get more difficult, more training is needed. We wouldn't train a child to fly an airplane just by throwing him in the seat and saying, "Okay, fly." That child needs training first. We have to make our work demands age appropriate, offer the training they need, and using common sense.

One of the best things we can do to prepare teens for the future is to put them through mock job interviews. At the ranch, they create a resume with their parents. We teach them to look the person they're talking to in the eyes, to sit up straight in a chair and not to slouch, and to always shake hands firmly, girl or boy. We teach them how to confidently meet people, especially when interviewing for a job.

Through the years, I have carried out tough mock interviews with our high school seniors because they need to be ready. "Hello, Mr. Jones. It's so nice to meet you. Thank you for meeting with me about the opportunity to possibly join your company. Here is my resume."

"OK, so you grew up in a children's home," I would say. "Tell me why I should hire you. Why are you different from the other 200 applicants I've seen today?"

That's when the teenager will look at me and say, "Sir, since I was twelve-years-old and arrived at the ranch, I have woken up every morning at 6:00 to do chores before school starts. I work very hard in the summer. I purchased my own car and will start paying rent and utilities on my own apartment when I graduate from high school. I'm self-sufficient. I will be an employee that you will never have to worry whether or not I'll show up. That is what makes me different."

You think an employer wouldn't jump on that? Of course! That's because someone taught that young person. They learned to be confident instead of slouching down with oversized thumbs from texting and playing too many video games. They learned a good work ethic. It's easy to look in the eyes of a teenager and tell if they've got "it" or not. "It" comes naturally to some, but "it" can also be developed.

In today's society, it is easy to think that we live in America, we are financially sound, and we deserve a new car, or the best shirts, or steak instead of pizza. Entitlement diminishes thinking and reasoning skills, and at the ranch, we think those are very important. Entitlement is a cancer that will destroy your child and family.

Your Example

Don't ever underestimate the importance of a parent's example. When our children see us arguing with our spouse over money, later in life they will do the same thing. If they see us sit down and work through money problems, and even include them in the discussion, they will be better prepared for life.

The conversation might sound something like this: "Tommy, we want to go to Disney World next May. It's December now so we are going to start saving money, so anytime we have any extra money, we're going to throw it into the Disney World fund. We don't expect you to match what your mother and I save, but you are going to take part of your allowance and the money you make mowing lawns to help us go." That may sound simple, but it will help train them to save and be a part of something much bigger.

So many parents will say, "Okay, you can do your homework tomorrow instead of doing it today." Uh, no! That homework chore must be done the day it is due, it's not something that you can put off. Their teacher is not going to extend their deadline another day. That college professor is not going to delay a test because they slept in. That will never cut it. The professor will say, "I gave you the test schedule and you knew it was today, so you have an incomplete." Children must learn that there is an obligation to get "needs" done before "wants."

Your child might say, "I want to go to the movies on Friday," and you respond with "Okay, you may go after you mow the grass." Then on Friday afternoon when they are getting ready for the movie, they can't say, "Well, I'll mow the grass tomorrow morning." As a parent, or preparer, our job is to say, "No, I'm sorry, but no movie. We had an agreement and you did not mow the grass." We must teach our children to keep their word as we will always keep ours. They must meet their responsibilities as we will meet ours.

Things to Do

The ideas mentioned here for training a child to handle their business only scratches the surface. Decide with your spouse what is appropriate for your child and then pursue it together. Handling their business appropriately is an essential trait in a man.

1. Your child will learn time-management skills by watching you in control of your schedule instead of your schedule being in control of you.
2. Establish a chore chart in your home when your children are young. Make a daily list of what your children need to accomplish. For example, it's okay for your four-year-old to pick up toys before coming down to breakfast. Chores should obviously be age appropriate. Boys are especially good at checking things off of a list.
3. Give your child a debit or bank card and if they overspend, allow him or her to be embarrassed in front of others. Being declined will teach a valuable lesson.

4. We are a debit and credit card society, but the simple math needed to keep up with a checking account is a great way for your child to understand finances. Teach your child to balance their bank account.

5. Make a ceremonial visit to a bank with your child and open a savings account for the child. Whenever your child has money, I would suggest splitting it 70 percent for savings, 10 percent for tithing, and then give the child the joy of spending 20 percent any way he or she pleases.

6. Place an empty five-gallon water bottle near your back door. Use it to hold money as your family saves toward a vacation. Encourage your child to drop coins in the bottle as he or she earns or finds it. The child will be so proud to have had a part in saving for the family vacation and will enjoy it even more!

Encouraging Work

As parents, we also should look for those opportunities where our children want to work and accomplish big things on their own. Any guy reading this will remember what it was like to build tree houses or camp as a kid. The summer Brodie was about nine, he decided to build a tree house from a big old pile of scrap wood. He tirelessly worked on that tree house for days. I didn't nail one nail in it. I did get up there to make sure that what he was doing was safe, but that was it. He was so excited about it. He got a couple of boys that lived across the lake at the ranch to be in his club and this was their camp.

One afternoon he came and asked if I knew where he could find an extension cord. I found it for him and he ran it from our home basement to that tree house. At the time, I still had a 12 by 12 refrigerator I had used in college. He found the refrigerator and managed to pull it up into the tree. He had created his own little camp and even had a refrigerator! Those boys would sit up in that tree house, laughing and playing. You could hear them thoroughly enjoying what they had built. That was the beginning of his love for building and planning, which to this day he does in his own home.

When Brodie was in college at the University of Alabama, he decided to room with three young men in a house. The three guys were going to live upstairs, but Brodie had plans for the basement. He called and asked Tee and I if we would come and visit him. We went and he stated, "I have an idea, what if we renovate this basement so I could live down here?"

"Sure," I said, so we sat down and figured it out. Tee went home and left me with Brodie for four days, and we bought the carpet, paneling, and ceiling tiles. This basement was completely rough and unfinished, but when we got through, he had a perfect little living room area, a bedroom area, and a bathroom. We constructed the entire living space.

"This was cool," he said when we finished. Brodie's not very demonstrative or verbal, but that "This was cool" was priceless to me because the work was something he and I had done together. The foundation was laid when he was young when I asked him to help me build things.

"Without consultation, plans are frustrated, but with many counselors, they succeed." (Proverbs 15:22)

Chapter 6

0 = One Purpose

*Purpose is an anticipated outcome
that guides daily plans and actions.*

In January 2010, the University of Alabama beat the University of Texas to win the National Championship. Before that game, Alabama had to win the SEC Championship against their nemesis, the University of Florida, for the opportunity to move on to play Texas. The night after the Alabama/Florida game, I had the privilege of being at the team's season-ending party in Birmingham. I sat next to Coach Nick Saban for two hours as he gave interview after interview with such ease.

When the meeting was over, my wife, daughter, and son-in-law asked me what it was like to sit and listen to him. "Just like sitting with Coach Bryant," I told them. They asked what I meant and I told them that it was evident Coach Saban has tenacious focus. At one point, he even looked at me and said, "Remember when it was third and eight, and we were in this particular defensive play? Florida was going to run the play and one of our guys didn't line up right. His feet were facing the wrong direction. He still made the play, but his feet were facing the wrong way." Coach Saban's focus was so clear that he even knew which way one guy's feet were turned in that one particular play. That is attention to detail, but that type of focus can also be called "purpose." You show me someone who has that kind of tenacious focus, and I'll show you someone who is very clear about his or her purpose.

Coaches recognize players who have clear focus or purpose about their roles. In the NFL, players only get a few weeks off from lifting weights, exercising, and running. This is especially true for quarterbacks because when they come into training camp that first week, they have to have every play memorized so that when the offensive coordinator calls a particular play, they already know the play and exactly where the wide receiver will be on the field. They have to be clear and know what they're doing, or they will fail.

Natural ability will get you through Pee Wee and junior high football, and it may even get you through the high school sport, but when you get to college, your competition will be against players from all across the country. Let's say you are 6'6" and weigh 270 pounds and have gotten to this point of your career with natural ability. Lined against you is another guy that is 6'6" and weighs 260 pounds, but his work ethic is better than yours. When you line up on the field and the coach calls a particular play, you ask, "What's that play? I can't remember," but the other guy steps in and says, "I know it." That player will make the play and score. Coaches or bosses recognize and use the players who work with purpose.

As parents, we have to know what our purpose in life is

before we can help our children find theirs. We produce what we are, not what we do. If we get it right between the Lord and ourselves, we will get it right in our relationships with our spouse, in our roles as parents, and as employees. Men, we especially will be great leaders in our homes. To be honest, that's the most important place where we need to lead. Win at home first!

As parents, we need a very clear tenacious focus on who we want our children to be. I'm not talking about what we want our children to *do,* but who we want our children to *be.* We need to be prepared, and have everything rock solid in our heads so that we can anticipate where they will be on that field.

I am frequently asked, "How do you build purpose in a young person?" I think the best place to start is with what the Bible teaches us. According to 2 Corinthians 5:9, "Therefore, also we have as our ambition, whether at home or absent, to be pleasing to Him." The simplicity of this verse is profound. We are either at home or we are absent from home, one of the two. Ambition is an earnest or cherished desire, and our one ambition is to be pleasing. There's the purpose. I wish my wife and children could tell you that in my every action I have been pleasing to God, but they can't because it would be a lie. I haven't pleased God in every decision I've made, and I have been foolish many times. There have been times my family has had to be brutally honest with me. On the other hand, we all have those people around us who will say, "What? You?" We shouldn't succumb to other people's criticism that tears us down. Two of Satan's best tools are guilt and shame. We must learn what it means to be pleasing and to practice it.

Coaches and Players

Our function as parents is to prepare, build, train, lead, guide, and direct our children. That should be our purpose when raising our children. "Train up a child in the way he should go, even when he is old, he will not depart from it" (Proverbs 22:6). Parenting is preparing, that's all it is. A head coach's job is to prepare his team to do their job. The parent's job is to prepare children to win.

The player, in this case, the child, has a job, too. It is to listen, to be lead, to have a tenacious focus, and to do whatever it takes to win. It's not always easy. I remember when I played football, offensive players would tell stories of Johnny Musso. During one game, Johnny had two broken ribs, was bent over and bleeding. In the huddle, the quarterback looked at him and said, "Musso, get out," But Johnny Musso grabbed the quarterback by the jersey and said, "Call the play." He wouldn't leave. In the huddle, the quarterback is in charge, but that quarterback wasn't going to tell Musso, a great athlete and winner, to get off the field. That same passion for purpose is what we have to train into our children. They understand it by watching us.

The player's job is to listen to the head coach all week, to take in all of the preparation, training, and practice. When he's on the field in competition, he can't listen to the coach anymore. He has to execute what the head coach has taught and trained him to do. That's what life really is. Our children display every day what we, as their parents, train them to be. For example, after our daughter, Reagan, had her first son, I remember telling her that she was a great mom. She didn't even blink as she looked at me and said, "Look what I had as an example." That is a testimony to Tee and the job she did.

How to Win

Success comes from teamwork. A football team has eleven men competing against eleven other men, but they are a unit. That's what separates great teams from average teams. Everybody does his job for the single ultimate purpose—winning the play. In football, you will win some plays and you will lose some plays. The bad news for you and me as parents is this: the two-minute drill to manhood for our children doesn't allow us much time to "run that play again." There's not a lot of time to practice. Our job as parents is to be prepared and to do our best to prepare our children for the plays they will face. When we know what the purpose is, we can anticipate those upcoming plays, be it alcohol, premarital sex, dating decorum, manners, respect for adults, work ethic, whatever. We need to prepare our children to win. We've heard a head coach say after a football game, "Well, that was my fault. We didn't prepare for that particular fake punt, or that particular play. That was my fault." And you know what, it was.

Brodie's first coach in the NFL was Herm Edwards. Herm Edwards is known for a lot of things, but the one thing he is best known for is a quote he gave at a press conference, "You play to win the game." That's it. We parent to win the hearts and souls of our children to prepare them for life. That's what parenting with purpose is all about.

Please allow me to give one more example from football. Our son-in-law, John David Phillips, also played football at the University of Alabama. He told me a story about Bill "Brother" Oliver. "Brother" Oliver was the defensive coordinator and considered by most to be a defensive genius while at Alabama.. He would always have the first ten to twelve plays scripted. He and Steve Spurrier, who was then at the University of Florida, would have a chess match for the first twelve or fifteen plays of the game. Spurrier would put a particular formation on the field and Brother Oliver would already have the defense lined up for that play. The next time Florida would run that same formation and Oliver would flip the play around and confuse the quarterback. That's all football is and that is what life is.

As parents, we can't expect things to stay the same. Things are always going to flip and change, but as the head coach, we can be prepared. The players have only one play in which they focus on, but we as parents can be ready for the next ten to twelve plays if we know the goal, the purpose. Each child will bring his or her own personality and responses to the play. Some will not follow the plan and will mess up, but you know you did your job in preparing them. Colossians 3:25 says that we each will suffer the consequences of our sins. We can ask for forgiveness and know that we are forgiven, but we will still face the consequences.

Some Major Plays to Cover

In parenting, like-mindedness is essential. Parents must be like-minded in the purpose on how to accomplish things. If one parent is a strong disciplinarian and the other is lazy and lets the child get away with everything, there will be serious problems. There has to be a unified approach. The worst coaching meetings ever are those when the head coach wants to go one way and the assistants want to go another and then undermine the head coach's plan for the game.

Good parental leadership is molding the differences of opinion and approach into one agreed upon game plan. If the head coach believes passing the ball will win the game yet the offensive coordinator ants to use the running play instead, they must agree or it's a sure thng they are going to lose. The head coach needs to know when to trust his assistant. The good news is that as parents we do have a check and balance if we are parenting with a spouse. The bad news is that if we are continually at war with our spouse, we will lose the whole game.

A Relationship with Jesus Christ

What is the main ambition, or cherished desire, we should have for our children? I think it is for them to know Jesus Christ. He's not a name they hear only when somebody messes up or hits their thumb with a hammer. He's not a bad word. Our children will know who He is and can come to know Him personally by watching us and observing our relationship with Him. They won't learn it from church activities, meetings, or missions trips. What they see in us, as parents in our homes (especially when they are between the ages of one and six) will directly impact the relationship they will have with Him.

With every passing year, the ability of our children to enter into a relationship with Jesus diminishes. When they are under the age of six, there is a banging on the door of your child's heart, with Jesus saying, "Let me in. I want to change you. I want to give you eternal life. I want to make you the best possible person you can be." Between the ages of seven and twelve, the banging becomes a very heavy thud. When alcohol, sex, power, money, and prestige start creeping in between the ages of sixteen and twenty, that deep thud becomes a strong thud. Between the ages of twenty and thirty, it might be just a simple knock, and as they grow older, that banging will become just a tap because the veneer of rejection has built up on the outside of their hearts. That door that used to be so thin and would allow in the clear sound from the knock is now covered in the falseness, fakery, and hypocrisy they see in our lives. The Bible promises it is never too late to come to Christ, but the question is, will they still be able to hear Him?

Our children can't be so bad that God won't come into their lives. They can't run far enough away from God that His hand is not on the other side trying to pull them home. It's never too late to come home. As a parent, we must pray diligently for the eternal destination of our children.

Brodie is featured on collector's cards as a college player and as an NFL player. All of his stats and performances are on those cards. His size, strength, body weight, everything is on the card. There are many people who read those cards and say they know him, but they've never met him. There's a big difference between knowing details about someone and actually meeting that person. The same is true in our relationship with the Lord. We can know all about Him without ever having met Him. Once you've met Him, it is a life-changing experience, and you can say with confidence, "I've met Him." We must do all we can to help our children actually meet our Lord.

Preparing for Marriage

Recently I watched a TV show about lions. A female lion had been injured and some hyenas were circling her. They wouldn't come at her face but would come at her from behind (they knew her teeth weren't on her back legs, hamstrings, or back). She was fighting for her life against the hyenas, but all of a sudden there was a roar that was so loud the camera shook. A blur flashed across the screen as the male lion came running to the rescue of his lioness. I had heard of "laughing" hyenas, but there was a hideous laughing sound coming from the hyenas. The cameraman never moved his focus from the female lion, but you could not miss the scream that came from the hyenas as the male lion took a swipe at them. Later, the camera moved to show that the lion had, in fact, with one swipe of his paw, hit one of the hyenas and broken its back. The hyena was writhing on the ground as the male lion killed it. Afterwards, the male lion went back and sat beside his lioness until she died from her injuries.

We don't see enough of this attitude or commitment in today's society (men willing to protect their wives without hesitation). Part of loving and cherishing is nourishing and protecting our wives, whatever the cost. It's something that is missing in young men today, and we need to reinforce that value into them. God instructs men to love their wives. It tells women to respect their husbands. God instructs us as men because we are weak in this area. We are to love and cherish just as Christ loved His church.

I know it sounds like I'm into lions, but I want to share one additional story that came from the same TV show. A male lion had been wounded in a fight with another male, and the hyenas were coming for him. The female lion straddled the male and would not allow the hyenas to get close to them. She stayed until he got his strength back and was able to stand up again.

I've used this example with the boys at the ranch to show them that there will come a day when they have been wounded and feel hurt and they will need their "lioness" to stand there beside them until they can get up and move again. They will need to know that she will never leave, betray them, quit on them, and will fight to the end. That's what they should look for in a wife, but they won't find her until they become the male they need to be. When the "hyenas" come prowling to hurt their families, be it the economy, immorality, illness, or whatever, they will be able to withstand it together.

Many years ago, I heard the story of the well-known minister E. V. Hill and his wife, whom he named, Baby. During his wife's funeral, he preached one of the best examples I've have ever heard of a wife's love for her husband. Mr. Hill was involved in the Civil Rights Movement in the 1960's when he received a threatening phone call during the night. The next morning he awoke, his wife was gone. He went through the house calling her name and found no answer. He went into his study and asked, "God, are you going to leave, too?" He then heard the kitchen door open as his wife walk in, dressed in her bathrobe and slippers. She looked at her husband and said, "I had a dream that they put a bomb in your car. I drove it around to make sure it was okay for you to drive."

It's equally important to teach our daughters the same principle. Reagan knew how to choose a husband who knew his purpose because she knew hers. One of the strongest things we can teach our daughters is to know who they are and to ask God to help them to become Godly young women who will attract Godly young men. Notice I didn't say a Christian young man. I said a Godly young man.

Parent/Child Relationships

When Brodie and I went to Alaska and we talked about manhood, I told him there would be some new ground rules from that point on. I knew that both he and I would make mistakes in the future. I promised him that we would get through them whatever they were, but I asked him to never lie to me, and to be straight up no matter what. I then made some promises to him, "I will not come unglued. I will not scream. I will not yell or get mad, and together, we'll work through whatever you tell me. From this day forward, when you mess up, you are to call me, not your mom."

Now, for those of you who are single moms right now, I'm sure you are thinking, *I don't have that,* and I am so sorry you don't. Or, maybe even worse, for some of you, your husband doesn't choose to have this type of relationship with your son. I recognize that you, too, have a tough role. Never, ever forget the deep soul-stirring inspiration you are to your child as that single parent or as a parent who is carrying a torch for the Lord. Yes, there may be some things you are not able to give your child, but never underestimate the power you possess as that one parent who stood by, who trained, and who prepared your child to the best of your ability. The truth will always win out. Parenting, or the lack of it, will always be revealed in the end.

For Brodie and me, from that point on, he knew that when he messed up, he was to call me, and he and I would deal with it. I would handle his discipline until he graduated and was a man on his own. The understanding in our home from that point on was whenever Brodie would call and ask to speak to me, my wife would swallow hard and say, "It's for you," and then go and pray that he hadn't killed somebody or done something really stupid.

The point was Brodie had to tell me what he had done. We got through them all, and to this day, there are things he has told me that I have shared with no one. I will never betray that trust. There are also things that I know he did that he doesn't know I know! But you know what? They were minor.

As a parent, we sometimes need to let those minor things slide and deal only with the major incidents. We can't always be in our child's face or riding their backs. Sometimes the relationship is worth more than the correction.

When parents ask me how to correct rebellion in their child or help them understand rules, I always tell them that those issues are not what they need to work on. The relationship is what needs work. Rules without relationship equal rebellion. If we get the relationship right, the rules will become clear and the rebellion will be diminished.

One of the best ways to evaluate our relationships with our children is to look at their willingness to talk with us. Some children are quiet while some are very verbal. Usually, Reagan is a lot more verbal than Brodie, but when you get him talking, he will talk, share, and be very direct. There have been other times when I've been talking with them both and they just sat, looked, and listened. Eventually, Reagan might tell you what she was thinking while Brodie would just say, "Okay." That's just the personality of the two different children. You have your own children who have very different personalities. Isn't it strange how children who were born from the same parents can be so opposite? Only God understands it, but He will give us the wisdom we need to develop those relationships if we ask for it.

I encourage parents to begin early working on their relationships. Consider taking your little girl to McDonalds every Thursday for breakfast, just the two of you. Take your twelve-year-old son who loves cars to a race and ten years later he will come back to you and say, "Dad, do you remember when you took me to the race, and I got to sit in the grandstands? I'll never forget that day!" Your son will remember that you didn't especially like racecars, but that you loved him more.

The best personal example I can give is that my wife does not like horses. In fact, she is scared to death of them! But I've seen her literally, with trembling hands, hold a horse still so our daughter or son could get up on the horse, trim hooves, , or do whatever the task was. She loved her children more than she feared horses.

When children are between the ages of one and six, we lay the foundation of our relationship. Between the ages of seven and twelve is the best time to invest in the relationship. After that, we start losing ground because their friends become more important. What they are doing becomes more important. During these early years we need to prepare them for those fake field goals that will come. That fourteen-year-old girl will be prepared when an eighteen-year-old boy is hitting on her and she isn't sure what to do. It's then that she will remember the time she was ten and you talked with her about what to do when boys expressed an interest in them. It's the exact equivalent of a coach preparing ahead of the game.

Respectful Obedience

Many parents are teaching their children how to count. When a parent says, "You need to get up and come with me. One, two, three . . . ," all that a child is learning is how to count. Your goal should not be teaching the child to count but to respond to your first request. Many parents see this as a form of grace, but it isn't grace. Grace, in this situation, would be to say, "Billy, come on. Let's go." If Billy continues to sit and doesn't follow, then it's time to say, "Billy, let's go!" Get his attention not because he's looking at you but because he's listening and follows you. He should not return his focus back to the TV or whatever held his attention.

Counting is not the best way to encourage obedience

and does your child a disservice. An employer in the future isn't going to say, "Hey, Ben, come here. One, two, three . . ." I know from personal experience their teachers won't say it to them either. My wife is a brilliant Calculus and Algebra teacher. I jokingly call her "Sink or Swim." She doesn't coddle, nor will most good teachers in high school or college.

Delayed obedience is a form of rebellion, pure and simple. Don't ever mask it under the guise of, "Well, he was busy." No! The child simply chose not to listen and obey. Isn't it funny that they didn't hear you before you got to three? Trust me. Normally, the child heard your request the first time.

On the other side of this equation, as parents, we have to show the same amount of respect to our children. If your children come in and say, "Dad, Dad!" and we are too focused on a football game or a book to respond, we too show them little respect. They shouldn't have to ask us four or five times to listen to them. It is a two-way street.

Delayed obedience is rebellion, pure and simple.

Honestly Recognizing Gifts

Great coaches adjust. A coach will have a game plan, but if he has a fullback who is not fast but will always get that one yard when it counts then he is going to create a play to get the ball to that fullback whenever he needs that one yard. That fullback is not going to be a breakaway threat, but you know what, he will run through three players to gain that one yard. He's simply using the gifts God gave him. You need to recognize your child's gifts and help them to use those gifts that God gave them for His glory.

Things to Do

1. The greatest way to teach your child to pursue that one purpose is to exemplify it daily and consistently in your own life.

2. When you and your family are watching a television show and something comes on that you know to be inappropriate, show your child how to be Godly by changing the channel or turning off the TV, explaining why you did so.

3. Doing something for others with an unselfish heart is one of the greatest examples to use in explaining that our one purpose is to be pleasing to God. It pleases God when we obediently give our hearts, lives, resources, and time. You can find ways to do this that are unique to your family and location, but consider things like serving in a soup kitchen, raking a neighbor's yard, or fixing a household leak for an elderly friend. Look for ways to have a servant's heart with your child.

4. One of the greatest gifts we can give our children is to honestly recognize their gifts and interests while they are young. Perhaps you have a son who loves music and you love football. You really want him to play football but he wants to be in the band. It's time for you to adjust just like a great coach. Recognize your child's gifts and let his or her desire be pleasing to the Lord, honoring Him because of what they have learned from you.

"And we know that God causes all things to work together for good to those who love God, to those who are called according to His purpose." (Romans 8:28)

Chapter 7

0 = One Body

Teaching our children to choose wisely concerning their bodies is critical because all choices create circumstances.

Our daughter Reagan, a tall, athletic, and beautiful young woman, is a wonderful mother to three sons, played basketball for the University of Alabama and was homecoming queen her senior year. Others always noticed her looks, poise, confidence, and athletic body. When she was young everywhere we went, people would ask, "Are you a model?"

I am 6' 6" and weigh 220 pounds. I'm just a tall, skinny stick. Most likely, she inherited her 6' frame and high metabolism rate from me.

When people asked if she modeled, she would always respond, "No, I'm not." She heard the question so frequently that after college she decided to attend a modeling talent search held in our area. I think there were twenty-eight national agencies represented and something like twenty-six of them asked her to come back for a second interview. Her mother and I sat and watched her go from booth to booth as they all gave her their cards.

Elite Model Management pursued and contracted her to join their company. After a short time in New York, they sent her to Milan, Italy, to work. It was a big deal for a twenty-two-year-old girl from Alabama. In hindsight, I wonder what we were thinking to send our baby girl off to Italy by herself, but we believed she was ready for it, and they had guaranteed that she would be well looked after, and she was.

We practically talked every day, and Reagan would tell story after story of these girls she worked with who were literally starving themselves to death. She had such a high metabolism rate that she would eat a couple of hamburgers, fries, and a soft drink before walking to her next job and lose weight from all of the walking.

Her experience in that world was one of body, body, body, body. But it was wrong, it glorified the body. It glorified the mind-set of the more skin you show, the more provocative and sexual you can look, and the better the product will sell. It was like feeding a beast. How much is enough? Reagan's values helped her to soon realize it wasn't the life for her. It wasn't what God had put her on this earth to do. A day came when they handed her a cellophane dress and said wear this, but Reagan told them she didn't wear cellophane. That experience helped her to know that that lifestyle wasn't the one she wanted. Again, it wasn't what God intended her to do with her life.

The Battle for Our Children

The world works overtime every day to steal and destroy our children's self-worth and self-confidence and redirect their focus. One of the easiest ways it does this is to lie to them about their bodies. What the world says about the body is louder than the truth. *You aren't strong enough. You aren't pretty enough. You should be taller. You should be slimmer. You should be faster. No one will like you because this body part doesn't measure up.*

The world also uses subtle messages filled with promises. *Smoke this and you won't feel the pain of not being good enough. Shoot this and you'll forget that you aren't worth much. Drink this and your body will be stronger. Have this surgery and others will look at you with envy.*

These are all lies. As parents, we know they are lies. But if a child's confidence is built on the false god of *feeling* special instead of *knowing* that he or she is special, that child is likely to believe what the world says. The wise parents I know have taught their children that their self-worth is not built upon the distorted view of *how* they look on the outside but on what they *are* on the inside.

A Gift—What Is On the Inside vs. What Is On the Outside

At our daughter and son-in-law's rehearsal dinner, our future son-in-law stood and said, "As beautiful as Reagan is on the outside, she is even more beautiful on the inside." My wife did a great job teaching her how to be a godly young woman. Reagan grew up knowing where her self-worth was rooted. If, as parents, our whole focus had been on the outside of the package, the inside would have withered up and died a slow death. Their marriage eventually would have, too.

A proper perspective of the body is one of the greatest gifts we can give to our children. God gave them the bodies they have, and He gave them that body for one purpose, to house His Holy Spirit. The Bible is clear in 1 Corinthians 6:19 that this is true for all believers. "Do you not know that your body is a temple of the Holy Spirit who is in you, whom you have from God?"

He chose a body specifically for each of us. Any time our children abuse their bodies in any way, they are defacing and abusing that precious gift, the only bodies they will ever receive. God made it the way it is and His intent was not for us to spend energy and effort on trying to force it to fit unrealistic standards. We should lead our children to a sound self-worth that will allow them to do the best with what God has given them. Their attitude should be more like, "I may not look like him, or I may not look like her, but you know what? I'm okay. I'm just who God made me to be, and I'm going to do the best with what I have."

The world will do everything it possibly can to convince them and us to do just the opposite. In very subtle ways it suggests that we should do anything and everything we can to improve the original model. There are multi-billion dollar industries built on this one goal. I think the more accurate message should be to do everything possible to take care of the one body we have, because if we do, it will serve us well.

When I sat down with Brodie on our trip to Alaska to talk about the body, it was a very easy topic to discuss because we were both athletes. He was a high school football player at the time, and I had played football throughout college. Our bodies were important in playing the game we both love.

"You have one body that's been given to you by God," I told him. "It was a gift, and you get only one. Don't give it away to drugs, alcohol, sex, steroids, or anything else that would cause harm to it." Unfortunately, I was able to point at many of my own former teammates and friends who played football professionally as examples of what not to do. Where are they now? Some are dead from abusing drugs to enhance performance. Many are abusing alcohol to cover varying types of emotional or physical pain. The experience of my acquaintances isn't unique. The headlines are rampant highlighting players from all types of sports who end up dealing with these same issues.

Parents Can Make the Difference

Taking care of the body given to us by God includes getting appropriate amounts of sleep; eating healthy, balanced meals and snacks; respecting the role of drugs as something to help combat illness and return us to good health; and exercising as a way to strengthen and maintain muscles and joints. Everything should be done in moderation. The goal should be to take care of the body, taking care of who you are, not striving for an unrealistic goal of being what others tell you ought to be. Helping our children to be comfortable and confident in their own skin happens when they know where their true self-worth is based. That's up to us parents.

I don't want to sound like I'm preaching here, but for some of us, this may be a little difficult to swallow. Self-worth is learned, as well as a taught, attribute. If we choose to do things to our own bodies that are harmful, yet we hold our children to a different standard, then we lose our right to lead because we lead by example. We can't get on a child for being overweight and inactive, yet we haven't done a minute of exercise in ten years and enjoy our time on the sofa while being 100 pounds overweight. We also can't go to the other extreme. Are you the parent who is eating 700 calories a day, counting every bite that goes into your mouth because you are obsessed with having a forty-year-old body that you are forcing to look like a twenty-year-old body? The deterioration factor, the age factor, genetics, heredity, and the care we've given our body factor into where we are now. But our children are just starting their journeys. It will be easier for them to follow a good example and develop that good self-worth if we model it for them.

Take exercise, for example. Not only is it good for the body, it can be a wonderful way to spend time with our children. Do things together and build those great memories. Help them to exercise without even knowing they are exercising by making it a part of your life.

Reagan's dream was to play basketball for the University of Alabama. In order to get there, she had to practice. At night she and I would go to the basketball court to practice ball handling and shooting. Hours on end we did this to help her reach her goal of playing basketball in the SEC. Brodie, too, had a dream to play football on Sundays with the best in the world. He and I would throw the football every night after Reagan had left for college, getting him ready to play for the University of Alabama, and the NFL. I can't shoot basketballs like Reagan or throw a football like Brodie, but I can rebound and catch footballs with the best of them.

Our son-in-law loves to rock climb. He and my two oldest grandsons will take a day off and just go hiking in the woods to play. That's exercise! Cade and Will will not remember it as exercise, but they will remember the great time they had being with their dad out in the woods.

As a parent, we can choose: Am I going to lead by my negative example, or am I going to lead by my positive example?

Be Realistic

Setting realistic expectations for ourselves and for our children is crucial. Perhaps your son is 4' 11" and weighs 85 pounds and can't walk and chew gum at the same time. He's never going to play in the NBA, and you shouldn't encourage and push him into a false hope or belief that he can. There is a man who frequents the gym I use. It's easy to see that he is taking steroids. Sometimes he will have his twelve- to thirteen-year-old son with him. He pushes and pushes the boy to work on being bigger and stronger and in shape. It's obvious to anyone on the outside that the son just doesn't want it. He's not interested. I imagine it's because he sees his dad's obsession.

We must listen closely to our children to discern the activities that interest them, not those that you and I want them to be interested in but the ones that they truly desire. Once we know what they are, we can help our children set goals and then support them as much as we can. If you have a child that wants to run, find a local 5K that you both can train and participate in together. Keep in mind that we are all motivated by rewards. If a reward will help encourage a discouraged child, then offer a reward for completion of the goal. These activities will build discipline and self-worth. Your child will also see you modeling discipline and a healthy sense of self-worth. What they see in you as you join them will encourage them all the more!

I have to give credit here to my own dad. My whole life he told me, "There's nothing you can't do if you want to do it badly enough." Big Oak Ranch is a result of that kind of teaching, as well as God's obvious blessings and leading. My Dad built that into me. We now try to build that into every child at the ranch, and we purposefully built it into our own two children.

Nearly every child that has come to live at Big Oak Ranch has come lacking exposure to proper nutrition. Some come in extremely emaciated and thin and in poor health. Others come in overweight from a diet of sugar-filled processed foods that were not intended for a developing, healthy body.

We had one boy who came to the ranch very overweight due to poor nutrition. It was quite obvious that being overweight affected his self-worth and his self-image. He started working after his first year at the ranch. At the age of 13, we gave him a lawn mower/tractor and said "go to work." All during the summer months, every day, he would mow the grass, work, and sweat like a dog out in the Alabama summer heat. (On a side note, he made so much money through the years that right now as a sophomore in high school, he has more than $4,000 in his checking account. He's very wise with his money!) He now plays football and told me just the other day, "I wish I had played football sooner rather than waiting as long as I did. Because I was so overweight, my shoulders developed incorrectly, and now I'm stiff. I'm game strong, but I'm not weight room strong. I'm working hard with a stretch therapist to loosen my shoulders so I can lift more weight, get stronger, and play on Friday nights the way I want to. Man, I just wish I hadn't started so late."

This boy was overweight when he left his hometown and came to live at the ranch. Now, when he goes back to visit, people don't recognize him. The one thing he hears over and over from everybody in his hometown is, "Go back to the ranch. You look awesome." What they see is not just the physical change, but they see something in his eyes, his countenance. His self-worth and confidence in himself have been restored. It shows in how he takes care of himself. He now believes in himself on the inside, and it is showing on the outside. It's a cycle. You've got to jump in there somewhere. I challenge you to start on the inside and the outside will eventually take care of itself.

The Body from a Man's View

While in Alaska, Brodie and I also talked about the way God created us as men to be visually oriented when it comes to the body. Men are built with a desire to look. But men, we must ask ourselves and teach our sons to ask where and why are we looking? Are we simply looking for a body that fits the Hollywood image on the outside with nothing on the inside? Or, are we teaching them to look at what's on the inside? The world holds up false images of what women and men should look like. Not every boy has a Mr. Olympia physique and not every girl has a model's body. God just doesn't create us all like that.

It's also crucial for us to teach our daughters to respect the male's visual orientation. I tell the girls at the ranch that as men we can't handle it when a female wears a blouse that's tight-fitting or pants that are too short. When a boy's body is shifting into the teenage years, that hormone valve flips on and his mind will race with all of the things he has heard other guys say or that he has seen on TV, movies, or magazines. We need to teach our boys how to handle this and teach our daughters to be respectful of what goes on in a boy's mind. Sadly, the opposite is also true.

When he was a teenager, I told Brodie, and still tell the boys here at the ranch, that there is a queen out there for you. You need to literally view girls as someone's queen because there is someone out there looking at your queen. I ask the boys if their thought of girls is how can I to get them into bed or is this someone to nurture and cherish as a great wife. God never puts queens with jerks. He never puts kings with a joke. You will attract what you are. You can't act like a jerk and expect the queen. It just doesn't work that way.

Another thing I tell the guys at the ranch is that I understand that they each want a good-looking woman for a wife. Absolutely. But, you know what? That good-looking woman may not be as good-looking in forty years as she is now. What she is on the inside is what will last, and the young woman who is confident and has a healthy sense of self-worth will pass on to her children. That is beauty that will last a lifetime and will only improve with age. As a parent, what we battle every day is what was once abnormal is now considered normal. When Janet Jackson had the infamous "wardrobe malfunction," kids twenty-one and under said no big deal while parents were aghast. It's all a matter of perspective, just because the world says it is normal doesn't make it right.

Other Harmful Pursuits

It's not just the sexual image that can cause problems for our children. It is the pervasive message that things that are obviously harmful are okay. The cigarette package says: *May cause cancer.* It is there for a reason! It means that smoking cigarettes is not okay. This also applies to smokeless tobacco.

Have you ever taken a drag on a cigarette? Not a puff in your mouth, but a drag. What did your body do? I remember practically being blinded because my eyes teared up so badly. My body was saying, "Not in here!" Your body will respond in the same way to most things that are harmful.

I was sitting with Brodie and his wife recently in a doctor's waiting room. There was another professional athlete waiting, too. Brodie was talking with him about the different sport he played. I sat and looked at the guy while he and Brodie talked. There was something different about him. I didn't know what it was; I just knew that there something was different. When he left the room, Brodie told me that the guy was on the performance-enhancing drug, human growth hormone (HGH). I asked how he knew, and Brodie began describing some of the tell-tale signs. It all made sense. I'm not a medical expert, but I do know that HGH is not a good thing for the body. I saw the outward evidence of the drug in that waiting room that day.

There is subtleness and a socially acceptable use in today's society of many things that are unnatural to the body, like performance-enhancing drugs, energy drinks and other highly caffeinated drinks. They give you a buzz and a rush. It may work for a little while, but then the body starts needing more. One energy drink just won't work. In fact, the instructions on the bottle say that if you want to have just a mild upswing, drink half of the bottle. If you want the maximum burst of energy, drink the whole thing. Hello! We have to stop and think about what we are doing to our bodies that has become, I dare say, addictive.

It's not okay to abuse alcohol, prescription drugs, steroids, performance-enhancing drugs, or other forms of illegal drugs. There is a reason that they are illegal. There is a reason why so many wrecks involving teens also involve alcohol or drugs. Society is telling us a lie. These things are harmful, and even though our children think they won't be tempted by them, once they go there, it's difficult to say no the next time.

I talked with a young man in jail and asked him about

the allure of meth. "I feel like superman for three days," he told me. "Once you go there, it's hard to leave it. I'm doomed for this lifestyle." He has made his choice. He wasn't immune to the lie.

Looking for Motivating Influences

As parents we have to be wise as we look for the motivating influences in our children's' lives. If the child has crooked teeth and is self-conscious about them, if possible, by all means, get braces for his teeth. If your child has a birthmark that could become cancerous at some point, by all means, have the birthmark removed. If your child broke her nose and it's now crooked, have the nose repaired. These are all examples of what you would call "no-brainers." There is a difference in intervening for your child on situations like these. Wisdom will allow you to avoid knee-jerk responses to society's demands that aren't in your child's best interest. If coaches are demanding players to take steroids in order to play a sport, you need to contact the police. Your child's health should always come before society's pressure of bigger, faster, stronger, and prettier.

Ask God to give you a thermometer to measure motivating influences. Ask: *What are the motives behind the request?* Be alert to those things coming down the road that want to change your son or daughter into something unnatural. Ask God to give you the wisdom to intervene when you know something is wrong. At the first sign of a problem such as your daughter excuses herself from the dinner table every evening to go straight to the bathroom and returns wiping her mouth, do something about it. Don't wait. Only a fool will sit and let his or her child slowly kill themselves because they didn't address the issue of caring for the body.

Things to Do

1. The greatest way to show your child how to care for his or her body is to take care of yours. Evaluate your own habits. In what ways do you not take care of your body? In what ways do you show that you worship your body by taking things to the extreme? Are the habits that you choose producing a healthy body? Be honest about anything that is dishonoring to the body and fix it. Children do listen with their eyes.

2. Take a walk around the block every day with your child. You will find two benefits; exercise and quality time spent talking with your child.

One Who Honored His Body

Think back to the Old Testament story of Daniel. King Nebuchadnezzar of Babylon had taken Daniel, along with thousands of others, into captivity. Daniel was among an elite group of captive young men from the royal family and nobility of Judah. The Bible says that he and the other young men were chosen because they were handsome, without physical defect, were well informed and quick to learn and, most of all, qualified to serve in the king's palace. They were to be trained and groomed for three years and then enter the king's service. The king wanted and chose for himself the best of the best.

King Nebuchadnezzar assigned a portion of food and wine from his own table to be given to these young men every day. The Bible says, "Daniel resolved not to defile himself with the royal food and wine." I find it very interesting what he chose instead. Talk about extreme self-worth and personal confidence! Daniel asked an official who had shown him favor to give him and his friends nothing but "vegetables to eat and water to drink." He asked the official to then compare his appearance and that of his friends at the end of ten days with the young men eating the royal food and to then treat them accordingly. The official agreed and fed Daniel vegetables and water for ten days.

"At the end of the ten days they looked healthier and better nourished than any of the young men who ate the royal food. So the guard took away their choice food and the wine they were to drink and gave them vegetables instead. To these four young men God gave knowledge and understanding of all kinds of literature and learning" (Daniel 1:15–17).

God honored Daniel's determination to obey Him and Daniel's refusal to defile the body God had given him. God has given each of us one body. We get to choose how we will use it. However, one thing is certain; God honors those who take care of that body. Where did Daniel get that confidence? He got it from the same source available to our children, parents who prepared him and a God He trusted.

"Don't you know that you yourselves are God's temple. . . . God's temple is sacred, and you are that temple." (1 Corinthians 3:16–17)

Chapter 8

D = Don't Ever, Ever, Ever Give Up

Parents give their children an immeasurable character trait by teaching them that commitment is a choice, and so is giving up.

In my sophomore year at the University of Alabama, we were playing the University of Miami. They had a great running back named Chuck Foreman. He was All-World in college and just an all-around great football player. He went on to play for the Minnesota Vikings and to have a great NFL career. At the time, our team had more offensive and defensive athletes, and an all-around better team, but there was no denying that Miami had a great player in Chuck Foreman.

During the game, Miami ran a quick pitch to my side. Foreman was coming wide, and I was trying to fight off the two blockers. One blocker was holding my jersey and pushing me. The other had his helmet in my ribcage. They were trying

119

to bury me in the ground, but I was trying to stay on my feet and grab Foreman at the same time. Back then I was weak in many ways, but my hands were strong. I had a good grip with my left hand as he was ready to make the turn. As he turned to run up the field, my little finger was caught in his jersey, causing that finger to be pulled sideways. I could feel that not only was the finger being pulled, but it was slowly being pulled out of its joint. It wasn't a jerk, it was a slow pull, which is very, very painful.

I had a choice, hang on or let go. I chose to hang on, because I had to. It was my job, it's what I was built to do, trained to do, and it was what I wanted to do. It was painful, but I had to hang on. I pulled Foreman down and made the play. As I came off the field, Coach Bryant said, "Good job." That's all he said, but that was all I needed to hear. I looked down at my hand and my little finger was turned 90 degrees to the left, that is why it looks the way it does today. My knuckle is about four times bigger than it should be, and when I place my hand palm down on a flat surface, my little finger will not lay flat. In fact, both of my little fingers look this way. I dislocated my right little finger in a high school game and the left one in that college game with the University of Miami.

Once I saw that it was out of joint I just pushed it back into the joint, straightened it out, tore a piece of tape from my wrist, and wrapped the tape around my fingers. I had a job to do. Now, this is not me beating my chest and saying look what a big, tough guy I am. That's not my point at all. Guys play with much worse injuries than a little finger out of joint. But, it is a choice factor. I chose to hang on and not let go.

Is Quitting Part of Your Makeup?

You may be the product of a mom or a dad who let go. Perhaps they let go of their marriage, their own integrity, or of their own children. Are you a grown man who spent his entire adolescence hearing your mother say, "You're just like your father," as she beat you? Her bitterness and anger was toward her husband, but you, as a little boy, looked like your dad and bore the brunt of her hatred. I've seen this scenario many more times than you can imagine.

As parents, we need to take a close look at our own lives to identify those experiences and influences that make us who we are and what we pass on to our own children. The hardest part is to look and realize that we have a choice to pass character traits on to them or not. Let's create a visual timeline to look at this a little closer. Take a wad of toilet paper and place it on the table. It represents your childhood. It may not have been great, in fact, it may have been a mess. Next to it, place something to represent your teen years. Then place another object in the line to represent your young adult years. Keep going by placing an object to represent your life as an adult, as a spouse, and as a parent. Sit back and look at them. These are the things that make who you are and what you are passing on to your child. You can choose to get rid of these influences but if not, you will reproduce these same traits in your child. You may find yourself giving up, or instilling a deep feeling of rejection like you experienced. Perhaps you will create separation anxiety in your children because your mom or dad left you when you were little, and quitting is just a natural by-product.

Quitting easily becomes a chosen habit, as does losing. The first time you quit on something really important, it's tough. The second time is easier. Then it becomes easier, easier, and easier.

If you are a parent of a preschooler, you are at the beginning of this journey. You have a clean slate before you of things and events as simple as the preschool Christmas play. If you promise your child you'll be there, you should move heaven and earth to keep that promise. It's a matter of keeping your word. Now, if you have a flat tire or wreck on the way, that's a different situation versus you just didn't do what you said you would because you chose not to. Excuses should not even be an option.

When I was playing for Coach Bryant, he would say, "Gentlemen, we have practice every day. Either you are in the morgue, on the way to the morgue, in the hospital, or at practice. There is no 'I didn't make it' or 'I'm late.'" We didn't dare show up late or miss a practice. It just wasn't allowed. Most great coaches today operate in the same way, establishing priorities and sticking to them. For us as parents, we have got to make sure that our children know the priorities and know that they can depend on us to know what they are and live up to them. They have to know we will never give up on the family, our relationship with our spouses, or with them. Of course, there will be rocky days and arguments, and maybe even a time of separation, but our choice is to never ever, ever give up.

When a parent doesn't want to attend school events or games or doesn't want to be involved in the child's life, the child knows and understands the decision the adult is making in a real and definitive way. We underestimate how smart and intuitive our children really are. We can't hide the truth from them. Don't fall into the trap of believing they don't know what's really going on. They do.

We teach the kids here at the ranch the importance of not quitting by not allowing it. We tell them that if they start a sport, they play until the end of the season. There's no quitting. When they sign up to play basketball, they play. If doesn't matter if they decide they don't like the coach or if they don't get much playing time. It doesn't matter. They finish what they start. There have been times when we discovered the child couldn't keep their grades up at the expense of the activity. That's a no-brainer, obviously priorities have to stay in order and academic's is more important. But, here at Big Oak we're big on, "If you started it, you finish it." You, like us, may have to explain, "You have four more games. You must finish." Next year they may come back and say, "I've decided I like it and want to get better," or "I don't want to do that again." Either way, they will have been finishers.

However, we never use sports or other after-school activities as a tool of discipline. Let's say your son is the starting point guard for the junior high basketball team. You tell him, "Either you clean your room, or you're not playing in tomorrow night's game." He doesn't clean his room and it comes to war between you. His teammates are counting on your son to be there. We can't penalize the child or the team because he's being a rebellious member of your family team by pulling him off the other team or activity.

For years, the United States has ranked consistently as one of the leading countries in divorce. What a sad thing, especially because there is always a ripple effect on the children involved. Just recently the parents of a young girl I know divorced. The mom made unwise choices, as did the dad. Neither of them wanted anything to do with the little girl. Fortunately she had grandparents who stepped it, but what would have happened if she did not have them? She will forever deal with the attitude of "when times get tough, I can just quit." Hopefully, in the future, she will choose wisely, but she probably won't. She'll marry; have an argument or two, get mad and separate. Historically, statistics show she will repeat history. As parents, it's important for us to repeat the positive histories we have and do our best to weed out the negative histories. This definitely includes a tendency to give up when things get tough.

Encouragement to the Single Parent

Perhaps your spouse has decided to quit and you find yourself a single parent. Perhaps your mate chose to go a different direction with another person or a different job. You now are left to pick up the pieces of the rejection your child will experience. You may have joint custody with your former spouse. What happens when you are competing with a Disneyland parent? Let's say you are a single mom with primary responsibilities for raising your son. A Disneyland parent is the dad who shows up every other weekend for two days while you take care of your son for the remaining twelve days. Dad takes him to Disneyland, fishing, to a baseball game, or even to a college football game. They have a great weekend and then he says, "Alright, Buddy, see you in a couple of weeks!"

You are the one who gets to make sure he does his homework and chores. You are the one who teaches him to make his bed and be a gentleman. Dad has become a play-partner and not a father. You are left with the job of training and providing the child with everything that is needed to become a quality adult. Single mom (or dad): Do the best that you know how to do and let the child know you will never quit on him.

Tell him that one day he will look back and realize that those twelve days you had of training and teaching him will be what makes him who he is—not the two days in Disneyland. Sure, those two days were fun, but they did nothing to build character, perseverance, or manhood in your child..

Again, being a single parent is by far the hardest job in the world. However, rest assured that there will be a day when your child is twenty-three, twenty-four, or older and working, maybe with a family of his or her own, and the Disneyland parent won't show up as much while you will always be there. Your child will eventually understand that the parent that always gave them money and tried to show them a good time by buying their love and affection was not a good parent after all. . He will know that the real parent was the mom or dad who worked two jobs so he would have food, shelter and to also be able to participate in certain activities. He will understand by the time he is in his early or mid-20s. So right now, if you are competing with the Disneyland parent, just remember there will be a day when reality sets in and your child will fully realize that the other parent quit and made a choice to go another direction and left you and him. Two days every other weekend does nothing to build a good relationship or to build a man. You have the privilege of doing that. The smoke screen of hiding reality will be blown away when your child reaches maturity.

When Commitment Wanes

Let's say you and your son are going to buy a table to refinish. You buy it, bring it home, and strip it, removing all of the paint and varnish from its surface. The plan is to sand, re-stain, re-varnish, and seal it with polyurethane. Your work will take a $200 pile of wood and make it into a nice piece of furniture worth something more like $1,000. It takes little effort to finish it, but would be so easy to not complete your task.

Let's say that about halfway through the project your son says, "Hey, Dad, let's spend today working on the table and let's finish it." If you respond, "Not today, we'll do it later," you can be sure that there will be a day when he will quit asking and the table will sit in your garage, unfinished, for years. You can give him a life lesson by finishing something that you both committed to finish.

Now that's a long way from quitting or giving up on a marriage, but, you know what, it's the little things that will add up to the big things. When he is sixteen and the two of you decide to purchase a car that needs some work, you'll make a plan to rebuild, repaint, and do everything it needs to get it going. You'll both be really excited about it. You might be tempted though when it gets hard and he starts pestering you to abandon the project and just buy a new one, you may be tempted. That would be a nice thing to do, but for many reasons, you determine it's not the thing to do. You should have counted the true cost of restoring the car before you bought it. Like so many things in life, there will be those long and arduous tasks to complete a project. But by setting an example every day, you will demonstrate to him what really is important, and that's to never give up or quit.

I'll give you one more example. Let's say you never learned to water ski as a child and decide to give it try as an adult. Getting up on water skis is not the easiest thing to do. Some people hop up on the second or third time, but others never get up. There comes a time when that boat guns it and it is getting ready to pull you up out of the water and for the tenth time in a row, your body doesn't work right and you flip forward out of your skis. Your hip joints are aching and your nose is full of water. You are so exhausted. Do you keep trying when you feel like you could drown? The whole experience feels foolish, but your child is in the boat watching. When your child sees you floating there in the water, exhausted, you can choose to say, "I just can't do this anymore," or "Let me rest a minute. I'm going to do this." You will have the loudest cheer from your own child. Your child will see that you stuck to it and accomplished something hard. That "Don't Give Up" mentality carries over into life. The principle is the same whether it is refinishing furniture, rebuilding a car, or learning to water ski. You have the privilege of modeling for your child the attitude of never giving up, never quitting.

Teaching "Never Quit" at a Young Age

It's not hard to imagine a six-year-old boy sitting on the floor with his Legos spread out all around him. Or as a parent you come in the room to ask him to put them away and you hear the universal whining, "Aw, Mom!" Then, the child just half-heartedly gets the job done. When you turn your back, he leaves, giving up on the project. He gave up on the chore you gave him. He quit. At that point, you have a choice, you can pick up the toys yourself or you can call the child back and make him complete the task. An even third option might be, "Hey, look, let's do it together." You've required him to get back on task, but you've helped him, as you required him to finish the task.

What's going to happen when the child is a bit older and is working on a science project? Again, you will get to choose to what degree you will help. Notice I said "help" them with it, not "do" it for them. By requiring them to finish tasks at an early age, you prepare them for when they face those tough things as a teen. If you train them well at the early age, as a teen he or she will walk in and say, "Dad, Mom, can you help me with this? I'm stuck and I can't figure this out." There is a difference between seeking advice so they can finish the project themselves and asking you to do it for them. It's important to start them on the right path on a small scale when they are young.

What Quitting Looks Like

There's not a person in the world that did not shudder when they heard the story about the Italian Captain of the Costa Concordia cruise liner that ran aground. The captain of the ship left the boat before he should. He indicated that he was in a rescue boat directing rescue efforts. Meanwhile, the Italian Coast Guard ordered him several times to come back onboard so that he could tell them how many passengers that needed rescuing. He kept saying back to the Coast Guard officer, "I don't know. You tell me."

The Captain of the ship had a choice, to be the captain of the ship or abandon his responsibilities and be a coward. He chose to be a coward. At least thirty people died as a result of the accident.

Too many parents pretend to be the captain of the ship, yet they are sitting in the lifeboat hoping everything works out okay. If you are in the lifeboat and you are blind, or if you are thinking everything is okay when deep down inside you know it's not, you need to get out of that lifeboat, crawl back onboard, and climb back into the captain's chair, even though the ship is on its side. The ship will never be righted unless you resume your responsibility and sit in the captain's chair.

Things to Do

1. Look for age-appropriate projects around your house that you and your child can start and finish together so your child learns the principle of not giving up when it gets tough.
2. Teach your child this mantra, "Do it right, and don't start what you can't finish," and "Once you start, you finish no matter what it is, be it your marriage, your parenting, a backyard patio, or replacing tires on a car. You have to finish what you start." The greatest gift you can give your child is an example of not giving up and the expectation that they will finish what they start.
3. Set the expectation of fulfilling a commitment. If your child joins a sports team and halfway through the season decides it just isn't what he or she wants to be doing, require that they finish what they started. It can be a great lesson in being responsible.
4. If your child plays a game and keeps the commitment even when he or she isn't feeling 100 percent, that is when you go out for ice cream and say, "I'm proud of you for not giving up and playing even when you didn't feel well."

Focus Is Crucial

Not everybody can play football. Not everybody is built for the strain, the rigors, the pain, or the frustration. Not everybody is a Heisman trophy winner, and not everybody is going to be a superstar.

There are very few people that can truly identify with being a football player without having been there. They don't understand what it's like to have a cracked rib or hurting so bad you can't even breathe. Few understand what it's like to hold your left elbow against that broken rib trying to make it not hurt so bad so you get up and get back into the huddle. You line up and the guy in front of you is bigger and stronger, and he's crushing you in every play. You still get up, go back in and fight, even though you are hurt and you know he will knock you down again. But, at the end of the game, you can hold your head high and be proud that you didn't quit. He and his team might have won the game. He might have won every skirmish against you, but he will respect you? And you should respect yourself, because you didn't quit. You got up and kept going because that's what committed football players do. That's what great parents do. That's what, hopefully, we are training our children to do.

"For I know the plans that I have for you,' declares the LORD, 'plans for welfare and not for calamity to give you a future and a hope.'" (Jeremiah 29:11)

Conclusion

In April of 2011, Alabama saw tornadoes rip through the state killing 243 people. The first tornado came through in the early morning hours. Meteorologists immediately began warning that another line of tornadoes should be expected in the afternoon would bring even worse devastation. The Big Oak Boys' Ranch staff, after hearing the warnings, began to prepare and were ready when the second line approached. As expected, one of those tornadoes came to the edge of the property at the boys' ranch, but instead of destroying everything in its path, it lifted off the ground, crossed the property, and set back down, continuing without destroying our homes.

When the tornado had passed, the boys' ranch director, Noel Vice, received a call from a long-time friend with the message that his parents, who lived a few miles from the ranch, were okay, but had lost their home. He immediately left to find them.

As he approached the neighborhood where his parents, an aunt, an uncle, and a brother all lived, Noel found that the last one-half mile of road to their properties was totally covered in trees. The downed trees were so thick you couldn't even see the asphalt of the road. His adrenalin kicked in as he climbed his way through the maze of downed trees.

Where his parents' house once stood was just a pile of debris. His parents, who had miraculously survived the storm, had gotten into their pickup truck to stay warm while waiting for help.

Noel sent a text to the house dads at the ranch to come with saws and help. The call for help went out across the ranch, and within minutes the first van full of ranch boys, ages thirteen and older, and house dads arrived along with first responders. The second wave of men and boys arrived shortly thereafter.

With dads directing, the boys, without hesitation, jumped in and started clearing the road. Their first goal was to clear a path so that an ambulance could reach Noel's parents' neighbor. This man had survived but his injuries were substantial. Sadly, his house was completely destroyed. His back and hip were broken. Knowing that it would take a long time to be found, he had crawled to his truck in an effort to stay warm.

The boys could hear the neighbor's scream for help. His anguish created an urgency that the boys understood.

Our boys quickly began cutting a path and making their way through the debris to get to the injured man. After four hours of man-sized labor, our boys had cleared the road sufficiently for an ambulance to get to him.

The boys continued working throughout the night. Their work ethic was so effective and productive that local rescue squads and authorities asked them to help with other areas. Just imagine it, strangers saw a work ethic that is uncommon in today's average young person. Not one of these strangers knew the stories or backgrounds of any of these boys who were working alongside them. All they witnessed was the fruit of manhood exemplified before their eyes.

Where did these boys, who had previously come from

dysfunctional homes, learn such a strong work ethic and how to respond like a man? They learned it from the godly men who work at Big Oak Ranch and who daily apply all of what you've read in this book.

It's not a matter of knowing how to run a chain saw, wield an axe, or use a handsaw, 'it's training the boy to be a man and equipping him ahead of time to rise to the occasion when devastation hits where real men are few and far between.

After the tornadoes, I wasn't able to get to the boys' ranch until the next morning. When I arrived, I saw those same boys already back at work, running from job to job, even though they had but just a few hours' sleep. I wish I could explain to you what happened inside my heart, mind, soul, and spirit when I made the turn onto the ranch and saw dozens of teenage boys working like men. My chest exploded knowing they had learned to be real men from the godly men who are their house dads at the ranch. It was evident by the way our boys responded that our house dads had been teaching work ethic and manhood.

What I saw in the boys at the ranch that day was exactly what I had wanted to pass to Brodie those years ago in Alaska. I promise you, it's what you want to pass to your son today. As long as you and your boy are both breathing, you need to know it's not too late. Use the principles laid out in this book and tailor them to your situation, to your relationship. Develop your own game plan and start practicing now with your son for the two-minute drill. The game is yours to win.

What We Learned about Manhood from Our Dad

An Interview with Brodie Croyle and Reagan Croyle Phillips

Family time continues to be a time-honored tradition within John and Tee Croyle's family, especially now that it covers three generations. On a hot summer holiday weekend, together, the entire family was enjoying fishing, boating, and just being together. John's now-grown children, Brodie Croyle and Reagan Croyle Phillips, took time to relate their own experiences and views about how their father taught them the principles found in this book and how they now are passing them to their own children.

Reagan Croyle Phillips is childcare director for Big Oak Ranch. Reagan is a graduate of the University of Alabama where she played on the women's basketball team and was homecoming queen her senior year. After college, Reagan worked for Elite Model Management before returning to her home state to earn a Master's Degree in Social Work. She is married to John David Phillips, and they have three sons, Cade, Will, and Gibbs.

Brodie Croyle was an NFL quarterback that played for the Kansas City Chiefs. Brodie played quarterback at the University of Alabama, the same school where his father was an All-American and member of the 1973 National Championship team. When Brodie was a senior in college, he was considered one of the top quarterbacks in the country. Brodie is married to the former Kelli Schultz, and they have one son, Sawyer.

EDITOR'S QUESTIONS Are in **Bold**
BRODIE'S ANSWERS Are in Regular Type
REAGAN'S ANSWERS Are in *Italics*

Brodie, what special memories do you have about the Alaska trip your dad describes in the beginning of this book?

I remember him calling me in and telling me we were going to go somewhere, and it was basically my time to break away from being a mama's boy. I had always loved the outdoors and hunting, so I wanted to go to Alaska and go fishing.

Well, Dad and one of my best friends and his dad ended up going. We decided we would do our own float trip. We'd be dropped off in the middle of nowhere, get in rafts, and float down the river for seven days, catching fish all the way down. Dad and I had our tent. They had their tent. Luckily, we had packed enough food, just in case, but our goal was to catch enough fish and then cook them each night. We had enough food. We had water. We had everything.

But, that year the salmon run was low. Fishing boats just sat at the mouths of the tributaries and caught all of the fish before they even got into the streams. We didn't catch a single fish in seven days. We only had one bite in seven days. We totally missed the run. So, we decided to make it fun in other ways. We'd play football at night and act like we were hunting this, that, and the other throughout the day, which we weren't, but we would look for bear tracks where we camped—hoping we wouldn't see any!

Well, that wasn't very smart!

When we were flying back, we finally decided to start

reading books on this stuff, because now we were interested. They said, "Never camp where you see a bear track." It was in bold letters in the newspapers, "No Fishing." Everything we had done turned out to be 100 percent opposite what we should have done!

That's our family in a nutshell. My wife is five years into it, and she still hasn't quite figured it out. She's a big planner, and in some things we're very fly-by-the-seat-of-our-pants!

We're not always planners. We like adventure. We're prepared, but we just don't always plan!

It's an, "If it's going to happen, it's going happen" type deal. And that trip was no different. It was just a little more dangerous than, "Oh, you might see a snake" here in Alabama. There are lots of things that can kill you up there!

My fondest memory of that trip is what happened when our friends went home. Dad and I ended up staying for three more days. We stayed at this little bed and breakfast called Yukon Don's. I'll never forget it. I've still got a hat I got there. While we were there we chartered a boat for a fishing trip. Still didn't catch any fish.

Didn't the guide say that he had always caught fish?

He had never gone out and come back with nothing.

And then he took them out and didn't catch one!

But that was the most fun time of the trip because it was just my dad and me. It was the first time when it had just been the two of us on an actual trip. Obviously, I had spent the night away with him here and there, but it was our first real trip together, just the two of us. So, for us to have those dinners where it was just me and him and him to be able to tell me what it means to be a man and what a woman looks for in a man, which at thirteen I wasn't all that concerned about, but it makes sense now, was great. It was an awesome, great experience, and I'm definitely going to do it with my son.

Reagan, did your Dad do anything similar with you?
In a pure act of love from Dad, we went on a hiking and repelling trip in the Sierra Nevada when I was 18. Dad doesn't like heights.

Scared of heights.

I didn't say "scared" of heights.

He's scared of heights! He won't even get into a tree stand that isn't a ladder stand, no more than 10 to 12 feet high!

They're just not his favorite. The fact that he would repel with me was very special.
A funny thing happened the day we went on the highest repel we were going to do. You know how quickly thunderheads can roll in when you are in the mountains? We were getting ready to take our turn when thunderheads just rolled in out of nowhere. They wouldn't let us go as long as the clouds were there. Dad prayed, "God, if you love me, please let that thunderhead stay here." We ended up not getting to do that repel, so we didn't do the highest one! His prayer was answered!

Dad has always told me how important I am to him, and how special to him I am, and how I'm a princess and that my husband should treat me the same. It was a continuance of that. He's also taught me to be very independent and try things and not be scared. I guess that's why he was repelling, even though he didn't want to!

Dad is 6' 6", and I'm 6 foot. It's hard to find clothes to fit us most of the time. It's cold in the Sierra Nevada's during the night and warm during the day. Before the trip, we had found the clothes we needed, but on the way there, the airline lost our luggage. We had gone to the base camp and then from there we were to get into vans to drive to where we would start the trip. We had waited and waited to see if the airline would bring our luggage, and they never did, so on the way, the whole crew we were with had to stop at Goodwill so we could go in and get clothes--sweatpants and sweatshirts. Dad was wearing some pink jacket that was about four inches too short on each arm!

The moral of the story is don't go anywhere with Dad.

It was funny, and our pictures from that trip are quite humorous because nothing fit us. Everything was way too short. Neither of us was the best dressed there, but we had fun!

Growing up, how did you see your dad live out being a man?
That's just who Dad is.

Yeah. Selfless.

Completely to his core, it is who he is. I think God set him apart very early in life to be who he is. Relentless. Passionate.

There's no doubt Dad has passion for what God has called him to. As soon as he knew what God wanted him to do, that passion has never wavered, ever. He just pinned his ears back and went toward it, kind of like that gladiator mentality. "Nothing's going to stop me."

He was going to the right Source. It wasn't in his own power. I think he knew that. As an adult and a more mature Christian now, I can say, Wow! That's amazing. I think it's hard for men. Men struggle with pride because this culture teaches them everything's on your own merit--everything's in your own power. To still be that masculine man and go to the right Source, I think Dad just pulled that off seamlessly, whether or not he even knew it. It was just who he was and is.

Obviously she's the counselor and is more outspoken than I am! Ditto.

Can you share a funny story about learning an ethic of hard work from your parents?

My summer job was to work at the barn. I'd wake up, feed the horses, clean the stalls, work the horses, clean the stalls, and feed the horses. That was the day. I started when I was nine or ten and did that until I was fifteen and could drive.

One day when I was probably eleven or twelve, the guy who usually ran the horse barn wasn't there. It was just me and two of my buddies. Dad was showing some people around the ranch, and we were in the barn and had fed the horses and halfway cleaned up. We were in there playing hide and go seek. I remember I was on top of the office looking down. I thought it was just going to be one of those, "Oh, they're playing hide and go seek. Y'all have a good time." Well, that wasn't what we got. We got, "Get down, do your job. I'll see all three of y'all after work." I mean we were scared to death.

We had to go to his office after work that day. He sat us down and explained to us what work is, what commitment is, earning your keep, the whole nine yards about what being a man and what being responsible is all about. For me, it set the bar for where I was going from there.

Then I remember a day when I was in fourth grade. I had worn jeans to school that day, and we had to run the mile. I had forgotten about it. This was the one time in my life that I thought; *I have on jeans and nice shoes so I'm not going to win.* So, I didn't go for it. I remember Mom getting so mad at me when I told her about it and then her calling dad and them both getting so mad at me because I didn't have that drive, that mentality. I'll never forget it.

Those two incidents, I think, had more impact on my drive to try to be the best at everything I do, no matter whether it is a paying job or sports or being a husband and now a father. Those two incidents inspired me.

Would you say that your parents' expectations were high?

I think that's part of being who they are, who he is, but also, being a good parent is demanding the best out of your kids. Not driving them to the point that they resent you for it, but letting them know that it's not okay to be mediocre. This world is full of people who are mediocre and can get by doing this and that. We just always knew we were expected, if we were going to do something, to be the best. That's something Dad has always said, "If you're going to go after something, you might as well be the best." We just learned to apply that to life in general.

Did you ever feel pushed?
Never. Dad's not a screamer. Dad's not a yeller. He didn't get on to us all the time. Very rarely did he have to use "The Voice." Don't you agree?

Oh, yeah!

I don't remember him having to get on to us much.

I never remember him yelling at me or pushing us to be the best at football or basketball or any of that. If anything, he had to rein us back, but that was part of our raising. After they set the foundation, we started demanding that out of ourselves. For me, personally, if I didn't reach that, if I went out and played a bad game or whatever, I was the hardest on myself. The same was true of anything work-related.

Hard on us? No. They just said if you're going to do something, we don't care what you do, but if you're going to do it, be the man at it. If I had not wanted to play football, he would have been perfectly fine with that. If I had wanted to be a duck-hunting guide, he would have just said, "If you're going to do it, you be the man at it."

Not every child has that drive to be the best. How will you strike that balance with your own sons?
I think it comes down to a lot of modeling, because, Dad and Mom, that's how they still are. They can outwork anybody at their age. I try to model it for my kids. I don't always do the best job, but I tell them all of the time, "Remember who you are, who we are, and where you come from." Something may be okay for other kids. Some kids talk this way. Some kids say these things. And some kids act like that in public. But, that's not who our

family is. We're not going to be like that." Cade will ask "Why?" I tell him, "Because God has asked us to be different so we're going to be different." We try to move on from there by saying what they are doing is not wrong. They are fine. We're just going to act this way. We're going to respond this way to people and treat people with kindness and courtesy.

How did your parents teach you to handle business, to be responsible, and practice good stewardship?

Does that sound familiar? Take care of business.

Yeah.

Take care of business.

Those are some of Dad's favorite words ever!

I'll go back to the horses. That was my first deal of taking care of business. I was getting into showing horses, and I needed a new saddle with all of the silver on it to be like everybody else. Well, I didn't have enough money to buy one. I was like, "Let me borrow some money? Will y'all get me this? Will y'all get me that?" My first run-in with business was over the saddle. I showed in a work saddle with no chaps and wearing a straw hat until I worked hard enough to where I could buy my own saddle, and I could buy my own shirt.

It wasn't like they deprived us. I don't want you to think that. But they used it as a teaching tool.

Have you ever seen your parents' compromise?
Oh, good gracious, no.

Never. Well, maybe they compromise with each other.

Yeah, and that they are sixty years old and should be retired! They help every day with babies, and Mom probably works harder than she's ever worked.

She does.

And Dad is still speaking like he's 30 years old! But on beliefs, no, or letting us compromise on what our goals were. I mean it would be real easy if I go out there and don't have a good game and throw an interception in overtime and all of a sudden I'm so down, and start trying to change goals. No.

Never get too high. Never get too low. Just keep looking ahead. Dad says that all of the time. Just keep going. I think Mom is the backbone of so much of that in our family. Mom has always been very black and white. This is right, and this is wrong. There's not an in-between. Don't you agree?

I do.

She's a lot of that compass in our family. Not that Dad's not, but she is a lot of that stability in our family. Right and wrong, and we're going to do right—or I'm going to kill you!

It's interesting that you don't remember a specific act of compromise because your Dad tells the story of when he compromised in front of you, Brodie, and you questioned it.
Oh, the radar detector!

I know what you're talking about!

I had forgotten about the radar detector.

Yeah. Me, too! Well, as you can see, it stung him more than it did us!

Who or what is your parents' master?
God Almighty!

In what ways did you see that growing up?
I remember a time when I was young. I don't even remember how old you were, Brodie. Dad doesn't talk about this, but he was always the last one to get paid in the early days of the ranch. He would go a lot of times without getting paid, but mom was a schoolteacher, and we did have that income. But this particular time was at the end of the month. It was time to pay bills, write some checks.

I can remember Dad getting all of the staff together in that old, long and skinny office, and praying, "Lord, we're doing this in your name and for your glory, and we need You. We can't do this in our own power." I vividly remember it.

By the time the bills were due, there was money in the mailbox—mysteriously. We had no idea where it came from. Years, years later we found out who had dropped it and learned that the same person had done that several times because that person's mother had told them when you give money you don't give it for your glory. But that just showed me the power of prayer, the power of faith, the power of being called and doing what God asks you to do. He will provide, and He always did. He always has. Mom and Dad both have always stayed true to that.

I remember those stories, and that's happened numerous,

numerous, numerous times—even recently. Just out of nowhere.

That was just the first one where I remember thinking, Wow! God really is real! That has always stuck in my mind.

My most vivid memory is of both of them in the hard times we've gone through. I'm going to revert back to sports, with our injuries, heartache.

Disappointment.

And disappointment. They have never wavered. So many times I would sit there and ask *why is God doing this? Why is this happening?* But they have never wavered. They just always said, "Let's pray about it. Let's talk to God about it. Let's give it over to Him." I saw that in high school and in college. That was, I don't even know the word I'm looking for, but it was unbelievable that in those moments they're still that steadfast and that strong. Knowing that their hearts are just breaking for us.

As a parent, I can understand that so much more now.

But knowing that there is a plan, and it's not in our hands. That's something.

It doesn't sound like your parents sheltered you from the difficulties.
You can't shelter anybody when you've got 80 kids!

Not living at the ranch! That's something that my husband has made me aware of, even from the moment we started dating. I wasn't always aware of how much we were aware of the evil in the world, the awful in the world, the hurt in the world, that there are people hurting all around us. I think it just became so much a part of who we were and how we lived life.

I know for me, with girls in high school and in college, the trivial things that they would stress about, that they would just cry and go to pieces over, I didn't know that I was doing this then, but in my mind I was thinking, Seriously? Really? We're going to get upset about that? *Growing up, one of my best friends was raped repeatedly by her father. Come on. Let's put things in perspective.*

So, no. They didn't shelter us, but I also don't think they threw us out there to purposefully make us aware of it. They were just living life, serving in front of us.

How will you do that with your children?

You can't shelter. Eventually you have to let go, and they have to see the world. And, in my opinion, if they can see that while they are still under your roof, they've got a whole lot better chance of not going down that same path than if they hadn't seen it their whole life. All of a sudden they're 18 years old and they are in college and its like, Oh! Okay.

You both are such confident individuals. How do you think living life in front of you played a role in making you who you are now?

I think my husband is probably mad at my dad about this now, but Dad used to always tell me, you can do anything any boy can do. Like, if they can play basketball until midnight, you can play basketball until midnight. If they can run that fast, you can run that fast. Whatever they can do, you can do, and don't let them tell you otherwise.

Our whole lives, anything we did, they both were always saying, "You are the best at this. You're this. You're that." If I went out there in high school and had a bad game and threw three or four interceptions, they'd say, "Oh that guy ran the wrong route,"or"Oh, that guy just made a lucky catch." They just had a way of making you get over it.

It's never been about the game. It's always been about who you are.

Right. But, also, they are so proud of us that I don't know if they'd ever admit that we had a bad game! I don't think Dad has ever said, "Whew! That was a bad game!"

Well, Dad has told me every day of my life, he thinks I'm beautiful, he thinks I'm wonderful.

He never told me I'm beautiful! He has always said he raised us differently!

John tells the kids at the ranch that they have one purpose and that is to be pleasing to God. How did your parents pass that to you?

So much of what they did is just who they are. As a parent, I focus on that so much, making sure I'm who God asks me to be so my children can see that—more than my words. I feel like I could tell them things all day long, something as simple as be polite to waitresses, and then if I say something like," Could you get me some more drink?" that would totally negate everything I'd said.

My husband and I want to focus single-mindedly on pleasing the Lord, being who He wants us to be. I feel like if we're that, it will trickle down to our children, not only in our words but also in our actions. I think our parents could not have been more that.

Mom always told me that being a parent is the hardest job you'll ever have. It's about being consistent every day, never compromising on what you know you want to teach your kids. You can't take a day off as a parent. You can't take a day off from teaching them the right way. You can't take a day off from correcting them. We're really big about Yes, Sir, No, Sir, Yes, Ma'am, No, Ma'am. We can't teach them that five days a week and not teach them that on the weekend. You have to be consistent. You have to keep going even when you're tired.

You saw prayer play a role in the life of the ranch. What about in your family?

I saw it in some ways that Brodie didn't even see, because while he was on the football field, my parents were bathing him in prayer, every game, before the game, during the game, and after the game. Praising God for the good, the bad, and the ugly. They would still praise God. But he didn't always see it. I always kid him that he didn't really get where he is on his own. Mom and Dad through prayer got him there!

That's right.

He had nothing to do with it. No natural ability or anything.

They need to improve their prayer life! I got hit a lot. I've got lots of scars!

Think about how bad it would have been if they hadn't prayed!

No joke!

In the last chapter of the book, John focuses on never giving up.

That goes back to how he says if you're going to do something, be the best. There's going to be heartache. There are going to be hard times. There are going to be times when you don't want to do it. There are going to be times when you have on jeans and hiking boots and you don't want to run the mile, so you just jog. You don't win. Well, you compromised who you are as a person.

It wasn't about whether you won that race or not, it was about whether you ran your hardest.

Exactly. Everything in this book is valid, but it's not like we ever sat down and Dad said, "Okay, tonight we're going to talk about never compromising." It was just our parents living their lives the way you're supposed to live, leading us. You can tell somebody something until you're blue in the face, but until they see you do it, it means nothing. We've seen our parents live this entire book, day in and day out consistently our whole lives.

After college I was living in Italy and working as a model. At one point I had the opportunity for a pretty big job but was going to have to wear a completely see-through top. It was a well-paying job for a well-known designer. The stylist told me I would have to wear it if I wanted the job. I said, "I'm not going to do it." The stylist said, "Well, you are not going to have this job." I told the stylist, "Okay, that's fine. That's just the way it's going to have to be. I'm not going to compromise." To use that word, I felt like I could hear my parents in the back of my head saying, "That's not who you are. Be true to who you are. None of this matters."

Sure enough, I didn't get the job. The next day, however, I got an even bigger job where I didn't have to compromise. That was one of those moments where I thought, Thank you, Mom and Dad! *It wasn't who I was. I didn't feel like I had to do that to be somebody, or something else.*

I had a coach in college tell me that as a football player for Alabama you will be better than most of the teams you will play. In one of those games where we were a lot better than the other team, I didn't play well, but we still won. I remember the coach calling me in the next day.

"Son, never play to your opponent," he said. "Always play to a standard." It took me all the way back to fourth grade!

If somebody's better than you, they're better than you. It's life. You hate to admit it, but its life, and at some point there's always going to be somebody bigger, better, than you. But it always made sense that whatever you're doing, do it at 100 percent. If it's good enough, it's awesome. If it's not good enough, you have no regrets.

You can still look at yourself in the mirror and go to sleep at night.

It hit home because that was the way I had been raised my whole life.

Sports are obviously big in this family. What were you

taught about honoring the body as opposed to compromising the body?

Neither one of us is perfect by any stretch of the imagination. Mom and Dad never called us to perfection. They may have wanted that for us, but never expected us to be perfect, because we are humans. We sin and make mistakes. But, for us, I think that even in that sin and in those things that would "defile" the body, or weren't how we were raised, what may have separated us from other people doing the same things was the guilt, the standard, the "We know this is not what we have been called to be."

For my boys, yes, I would love for them to go through life and never make huge mistakes. But that's not life. We all make mistakes and we all make bad decisions. But, I hope for them, that they always have the conviction and that they always can remember right from wrong. That they will think, okay, I compromised, but that's not who I am. That's not where I came from. That's not what the Lord has asked me to be. At that point they can choose correctly. It's not that they choose wrongly to begin with, but that they can identify it and then choose correctly. I think that was it for us. We didn't always choose correctly the first time around, but we did know it was an incorrect decision and then would choose correctly. Do you agree with that?

Well said.

What would you say to parents pushing a child in sports?

Chill out.

I hadn't seen it until going to my nephews' games. Every kid isn't going to go out there and be the best soccer player or the best football player. When I talk at Pee Wee camps and places like that, that's what I tell them. All of you are not going to be professional football players. That is perfectly fine! God put us all on the earth for specific reasons. Mine was to play professional football and hopefully, eventually, be able to help younger kids, whether it's as a high school coach or somehow helping kids, or coming back to the ranch. I don't know what the future holds for me but, seeing these parents is actually comical, sad, but comical.

I appreciate this about my husband. It's not about whether Cade or Will score the most goals or hit the most homeruns. You know how they say you marry somebody just like your dad? I see Dad in him in this area. I see the same core value of our son may not be the best out there, and he may not score the most goals, but he's going to try harder than anybody else. He's going to run harder than anybody else, and he's not going to quit.

John David even corrected me and my mama's heart recently when Cade wasn't feeling good at a game. I kept saying, "Maybe we should take him some more water. Maybe he needs to sit out because he's not feeling good. Blah, blah, blah."

John David said, "Hey, some days you don't feel good, and you still have to get up and do what you're supposed to do. He's going to do what he's got to do."

If that's not Dad! "Oh, my word," I told him. "You know what? You're absolutely right." We made Cade finish. John David told him, "Buddy, I know you don't feel good, but you've still got to give it all you've got." And he did. He played fine. It's one of those moments when I was the most proud of him because he found that something extra down deep.

There are always times in a person's life where you find that you're a little deeper than you thought. You've got that extra little something down deep. That was a moment for my child when he did that. He just found that other level and that little bit of deep. He dug deep and finished, and he was proud of himself. That was such a time for us. We took him for ice cream and praised him. I think they even lost the game, but it wasn't about the outcome of the game. It was a matter of him pushing himself to that next level.

John David did a really great job of relating it to life, telling him, "Buddy, there are days when mom wakes up, and she's tired and doesn't want to have to cook breakfast and do all that she does. There are days when I wake up and don't want to have to go to work, but we have to do it. We have to keep going. We have to dig harder and push harder, and it's not just in sports. You'll use this. This is life."

Some parents are focused on the sport and not the core value of who their kids are. Whether it's cheating or whether it's fudging, it's just a matter of the outcome of the game. It's not about the future adult their kids are becoming. These are future adults we're raising. We're not just raising kids to succeed in kid's sports. We're raising future adults who need to be productive members of society, and hopefully, ones who find what the Lord wants them to do and have enough gumption to do it.

I've gone to games when I didn't even want to stand up and cheer for Cade because I was scared people were going to think I was yelling like everybody is yelling at their kids. The sad part is you can see those kids breaking inside because the one person they are trying to please is the one person yelling at them telling them they're not doing good enough. It's been a learning experience for me. Our dad never did that. I will say I'll never do it. I'll tell you I'll never do it. Will I have the urge or not? I don't know!

Well, I said I wasn't going to be that crazy soccer mom who, when her child scored a goal, jumps up and acts crazy.

That's you for sure!

I do. I'm so proud!

Brodie, how prepared were you to be a man?
I was very prepared, but you can be as prepared as you want and there are still going to be things that you have to learn on your own. Unfortunately, I was blessed with a lot of stubbornness, so I've always liked to learn things on my own. But, as good as our parents were and are, there comes a point where, as Dad will say, "Buddy, your bags are packed. From here on out you've got to learn it on your own."

After four years of marriage, I love my wife more than anything in this world, along with our son, but I'm still learning to be the best husband I can be, and I'm only months into being a father. I know that I have a lot to learn, the same way my parents had to learn. It wasn't taught to them. It was self-learned.

So, they prepared you each, but your life has been up to you?
You can't decide things for your child.

Any last thoughts?
This is a sentimental thought, but I tell my husband all of the time that I look at most of our girls at the ranch, and it breaks my heart because they've never had a man in their lives to stand up for them. They've never had a man in their lives to love them unconditionally. I think that for young girls, especially, and even

as a woman, we get so much of our confidence and self-esteem from being unconditionally loved by our father, unconditionally loved by that good man in our lives.

I've never understood why the Lord blessed me with three men who would die for me. I know that it starts from my dad. My dad would die for me and loves me unconditionally. He taught my brother to be that same kind of man who would die for me, I think, maybe, if we didn't argue! But then he taught me to look for that same characteristic in a husband. I wonder why I was so blessed, to have that when there are so many girls out there who are literally dying to have that in their lives. They're dying for a man in their lives to step up and be that for them.

That's what I hope this book does. I hope it challenges men to be that for their little girls, their nieces, or any little girl the Lord puts in their lives. Be that man for them. Teach them that they are valued and to look for that same characteristic in a husband.

107154

CPSIA information
Printed in the USA
LVOW040740131
307065LV

107154

9 781433 680717